Agile Metrics
Measure That Matters

PADMAPRIYA D

INDIA • SINGAPORE • MALAYSIA

ISBN 979-8-89415-298-1

Contents

Preface

"If you can't measure it, you can't improve it."

– Lord Kelvin

Humans are inherently driven to improve and shatter the limitations of the known and forge a path towards the impossible.

Measures have its roots for many centuries in the world. During a recent archaeological excavation at Keezhadi, India, a remarkable discovery was made – a measuring crystal stone dating back to 200 BC which serves as compelling evidence of advanced mensuration practices in the region as far back as 200 BC.

This isn't an isolated example. The Egyptian cubit, the Indus Valley units of length and the Mesopotamian cubit were used in the 3 BC and are the earliest known units used by ancient peoples to measure length.

These early systems highlight the universality of humans to quantify the world around them based on everyday experiences and readily available local objects.

After the 18th century, as the innovation of electricity rapidly spread across nations, the time had come to dissolve the localized metrics of individual nations. The world was on the cusp of globalizing, simplifying, and modernizing, fueled by the wave of industrialization that was sweeping across the globe.

Following these transformative developments, the field of information technology (IT) emerged as a prominent industry, with remarkable growth and advancement from the late 20th century into the early 21st century.

Despite the rapid advancements, the application of metrics in the IT industry remains neither simplified nor standardized.

This book is written to address exactly the issues of applying the Metrics in the IT industry.

Few basics questions answered in this book are:

1. What is metrics

2. Why we need metrics

3. What should be measured

4. Who should measure

5. How to improve the system using metrics

6. What is the difference between IT metrics vs other industry metrics

7. What are the latest metrics used by Agile teams

8. What metrics for newly formed teams.

9. What metrics can be enhanced for higher maturity teams.

10. Best practices for scope estimation for leaders

11. Measure using OKR and KPI's.

These questions weigh on the minds of every IT leader, and even with the help of AI tools, specific solutions to the metrics challenges faced by every IT organization remain elusive.

This book is intended for professionals who are involved in various capacities in the IT sector and hold responsibilities related to the implementation and management of metrics in their respective organizations.

Chapter 1

Delve into the significance of metrics within the IT industry and also examine the existing approaches to metric implementation.

Chapter 2

Speaks about the software team metrics for both quantitative and qualitative and also the ways and means of how individuals can measure themselves. Best practices of estimation are also discussed.

Chapter 3

While IT systems often focus on measuring the performance of teams, what about measuring the organization as a whole? This chapter underscores the significance of evaluating the IT organization itself and leadership metrics.

Chapter 4

In this chapter, we delve into the methodology of gauging customer engagement through the lens of Agile IT. We explore the intricate connection between Objectives and Key Results (OKRs) and Key Performance Indicators (KPIs) to derive pertinent metrics at the business level. These metrics are meticulously aligned with the market dynamics as well as the performance of individual teams.

Chapter 5

The author reflects on the critical role that metrics play in the IT industry and explores the emerging trends and challenges in measuring success and progress in an Agile context. This chapter provides a forward-looking perspective, addressing the potential synergies and opportunities for further integration of Agile principles with the measurement and management of Key Performance Indicators within IT organizations.

Please note that this book exclusively addresses metrics for IT organizations that have implemented Agile methodologies or are in the process of adopting Agile practices.

Basic understanding of the IT industry and Agile is necessary to read the book.

The true reward for this book lies in the practical insights and ideas it provides, which, when applied to foster the growth of an IT organization, become valuable contributions.

This book is a summary of the author's over a decade experience in agile implementation in various platforms.

By the end of this book, you will have a deep understanding of how to implement metrics effectively in your IT organization, and you will be able to use this knowledge to improve your team's performance, increase your ROI, and deliver better value to your customers.

Thanks to my dearest mom D. Padmavathy and dad Arcot Masilamani Devarajan, their unwavering love and support have been the foundation of everything I achieve. This book is a testament to their lifelong belief in me.

Gratitude to my esteemed Gurus, Vethathiri Maharishi and her beloved daughter Uma Vethathiri and Dr. Alagar Ramanujam whose guidance and wisdom have been a guiding light not only in my life but also proved invaluable in shaping the core ideas of this book.

Thanks to hubby Gokul for unwavering love and patience have been my rock during the long hours spent writing this book. To my amazing kids, Sangamithra and Prathumanan for your love and for reminding me the purpose of life. Your patience with late nights and stolen weekends is a sacrifice I will never forget. This book is dedicated to creating a future where you can pursue your dreams with focus and agility.

I have a successful career today and its because of my dear friend Persis veena, who provided unconditional support along with my cherished friends, Nivethitha Gangai, Thilaga, Hemalatha, Saranya, and Abinaya for your unwavering support in my hard times and countless conversations that fueled my ideas and the laughter that kept me going. There's no way I could have gotten through difficult periods without the unconditional support of my brother Adv. Aravind Raj and his amazing wife Adv. Sanjana.

To my amazing Agile team: Vani Suryaprakash, Shruthi Kulkarni, Ramakrishnan, Nadeem, Jayashree and Annapoorni. Your meticulous review of every single word has been incredibly valuable. This book wouldn't be what it is without your dedication and expertise. Thank you for making my dream a reality! Thanks to Notion press for publishing the book.

Chapter 1

Metrics in IT

"You can't manage what you can't measure."

- Peter Drucker

Metrics provides us with a vital feedback loop, allowing us to track progress, identify areas for improvement, and refine our approaches. Metrics origins trace back to ancient civilizations, where rudimentary measurements were employed to gauge progress in agriculture, construction, and trade. As societies evolved, so did the sophistication of metrics, with advancements in mathematics and technology enabling more precise and detailed quantification. Today, metrics permeate every industry, providing critical insights into operational efficiency, customer satisfaction and financial health. From measuring crop yields to cosmological research, metrics empower the world to make informed decisions, optimize processes, and achieve sustainable success.

Origin of metrics

We are living in a multi-dimensional universe, though the exact number of dimensions is still a topic of discussion.

In the process of evolution, from single cell amoeba to six sense humans, each species has the tendency to observe and measure for every thing which is involved to survive their lives.

Bird migration includes complex measurements of length and time. Do you think the classical web creation by spider web can be constructed without any gauge? Every species in the world measures but the unique thing humans do is ; measuring with 'numbers'.

Humans of the past measured length with human parts like foot, cubit, pace, yard, span and strides etc. They measured time with repetitive and uniform actions like 1 snapping of finger is considered as 1 second. In essence, measurements are tools created by humans to make sense of and interact with the world around them. These systems of measurement help bridge the gap between the inherent properties of physical objects and our ability to quantify and manage them for various purposes in everyday life.

Measurements standardized:

Length was measured as Rhynland rood in South africa, Setat in Egypt, ZHI ZHANG in China, Furlong in India. Later length measure was standardized as meter in the 19th century.

In various states in India, rice is measured using a container called Paili in Maharashtra, Aazhakku in Tamilnadu, Paseri in Madhya Pradesh, Sola in Andhra, Paavu in Karnataka and Para in Kerala. While these are place centric traditions in olden days when travel and multicultural living was a rare thing. All the above various rice measures are now standardized as 1 kg. More travel across regions after the 17th century enabled them to reform their unwieldy and archaic system of many local weights and measures and also practically easy when unified. Hence S.I units gave birth in 1960 and updated periodically since then to standardize the measurements all over the world.

Measurement vs Metrics:

- A measurement is a single, quantifiable observation of an attribute or characteristic.

- It's the raw data point, like weight on a scale (55 kg) or time spent on a task (2 hours).

- Measurements are fundamental, but on their own, they don't tell the whole story.

- A metric is a measurement in context. It takes that raw data and adds meaning by comparing it to something else, establishing a target, or analyzing it over time.

- It tells you how something is performing relative to a goal or benchmark.

- Examples of metrics: customer satisfaction score, website conversion rate, project completion time compared to deadline.

Imagine measuring your height (measurement) as 180 cm. That information alone isn't very useful. But if you use that measurement as a metric to compare yourself to the average height for your age group (another metric), then you gain a more meaningful understanding of your stature.

Metrics Etymology:

Borrowing from the Greek word "metron," or "a measure," a commission assigned by the academy gave the name "meter" to the unit of length. Interestingly, humans measured distance more than any other measurement and hence meter became measurement itself which resulted in the word metrics.

"science of versification," 1760, from Latinized form of Greek *he metrikē* "prosody," plural of *metron* "meter, a verse; that by which anything is measured: measure, length, size, limit, proportion" (from PIE root *me- (2) "to measure").

There is no absolute metric in the universe:

An amount of substance was decided to be considered as 1 kg. The quantity of 1kg varies for sugar, rice, pulses and wheat. Yet we have uniformed the measure as 1kg.

There is an important insight in this matter. By nature, stone, sugar, salt, rice, and wheat are made up of mass with various chemical components. The numeral 1 kg is a human-made construct, created to simplify and standardize the way we quantify and compare masses. Comparing masses and quantifying the mass is a relative approach not obsolete. Hence we can comment that not only for estimation but also metric is relative gauge for humans.

Why we need metrics:

Metrics are essential for any system that wants to track progress, make informed decisions, and achieve goals. Metrics are useful to benchmark the performance against competitors. In the current VUCA world, Metrics are essential to understand the change of trends in the market. To encapsulate, Metrics are important for improvement.

IT vs Other industries metric:

Quantitative and standardized metrics in industries like manufacturing are more relatable as they deal with tangible, physical products. However, this relatability differs in service and IT industries, which primarily deal with digital solutions. So any item can be taken and measured either in quantity (Mass, Length)and time where products are involved.

The IT industry deals with software which is intangible. Before we are measuring an entity we need to understand the entity itself. For example when electricity was discovered around the 18th century, the fundamental units were not enough to measure electricity since electricity was not a physical static product. Hence units like ampere, volts, ohm and watt were introduced to measure components of electricity.

Similarly, if we are in need to measure the IT industry, we need to understand 'What needs to be measured?' before determining the metrics to be measured. Like electricity, IT is also a complex component for measurement.

The IT industry plays a pivotal role in supporting and enhancing the operations of various sectors, ranging from agriculture to astrophysics. By leveraging computing technologies, IT addresses the challenges faced by these industries, transforming pain points into valuable features. Understanding and translating client requirements into effective code is an iterative process in Agile, not a one-way execution. Therefore, the core of IT lies in generating value through programming or IT solutions.

Maarten Dalmijn in one his article cites ' delivering a feature doesn't mean you will deliver value, just like telling a joke doesn't mean people will laugh. Focusing on delivering more features means you're like a comedian who focuses on telling more jokes. Telling more jokes isn't the point, getting more laughs is.' Hence focussing on value flow is more important than delivery in the IT industry which should be the first primary measure of any IT unit.

How to measure value flow:

To Measure the value flow, let's understand the value.

Combination of input and process determines the value. The quality, relevance, and efficiency of input directly impact the subsequent processes. The process, in turn, refines, transforms, and interprets the input to generate valuable outcomes. Together, input and process determine the effectiveness, accuracy, and significance of the values produced within the system. To summarize, different inputs or processes will result in different outputs with varying degrees of value. The rate at which the value flows from input to output is called Value flow.

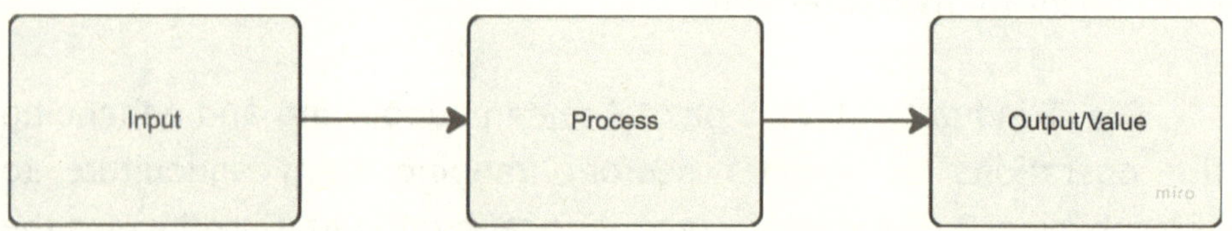

So it's clear that to measure the value flow in IT, understanding the Input component of IT and Processing ways in IT are important.

The 17th State of Agile Report from Digital.ai says that " 70% of respondents said IT and the software development and delivery teams use Agile, as do nearly half of engineering, product, and R&D teams. Year over year, engineering/R&D teams saw the biggest growth in Agile usage — just 32% used Agile in 2022, 16% fewer than in 2023.".

Above data shows immense growth of Agile in IT, hence let's take Agile ways of software development for further discussion in this book.

Agile is a set of values and principles grounded on an iterative approach for software development gifted to the world by 17 software professionals in the year 2001.

In Agile, Input of work, Process and output execution are inspired by Agile Values and Principles and guided by Agile frameworks like Scrum, Kanban and XP. Large scale agile implementations are shepherded by scaling agile frameworks.

Let's discuss the evolution of Work Input (Planning and Estimation) and process (Execution) in Agile frameworks which lead us to derive measuring the Value flow.

Scrum is now - by far - the most dominant framework in Agile. While Scrum has undoubtedly made significant contributions to the IT world, such as simplifying roles, focusing meetings, and emphasizing the value of artifacts, yet Scrum remains relatively silent on the topics of estimation and engineering practices.

Any teams that claim to follow Scrum for their planning and execution often incorporate estimation techniques from Extreme Programming (XP). This is because Scrum intentionally avoids prescribing specific estimation methods, allowing teams to adapt and adopt approaches that suit their context and preferences. XP's estimation practices, such as Planning Poker and T-Shirt sizing, have gained popularity due to their simplicity, collaborative nature, and ability to handle uncertainty.

Origins of common practices in Agile planning and estimation:

- Scope decomposition to User Stories originate with Extreme Programming, their first written description in 1998 only claims that customers define project scope "with user stories, which are like use cases".

- 2003: the INVEST checklist for quickly evaluating user stories originates in an article by Bill Wake, which also repurposed the acronym SMART (Specific, Measurable, Achievable, Relevant, Time-boxed) for tasks resulting from the technical decomposition of user stories.

- 2004: the INVEST acronym is among the techniques recommended in Mike Cohn's "User Stories applied", which discusses the concept at length in Chapter 2.

- In need of prioritizing and forecasting, The concept of story points was originally developed by Ron Jeffries around 1999 as part of the Extreme Programming (XP) agile framework.

- In 2002, James Grenning created planning poker commonly referred to as "scrum poker". Later, Mike Cohn, co-founder of Agile Alliance and Scrum Alliance, popularized the technique in his book Agile Estimating and Planning(2005).

- Sum of the story points completed in a sprint is termed as velocity. The term velocity for Agile was first written by Kent Beck and Martin Fowler in their book Planning Xtreme programming, (2000). Its interesting to cite that the authors have not prescribed 'Velocity' for teams rather for individuals in the book.

- 2001: the "role-feature-reason" format for expressing user stories is invented at Connextra in the UK

- 2002: The Scrum community picks up the practice of measuring "velocity" for teams prediction based on story points.

To measure the value flow of a team a new formula is proposed based on velocity as below:

Value Flow of a team = Average Velocity of team /Impediments of team

Average Velocity = Velocity of teams in last 3 sprints/3

Now, the immediate question to ponder is 'How to compute numerical value for impediments?'

Here is the solution:

Take the list of impediments of the team and assign the relative story points in fibonacci series for the impediments which pertains for that sprint.

let's assume a team is having 5 impediments, Based on complexity to resolve assign the impede points say

Impediment 1 → 13 impede points

Impediment 2 → 3 impede points

Impediment 3 → 2 impede points

Impediment 4 → 5 impede points

Impediment 5 → 2 impede points

Now total the impede points 13+3+2+5+2 =25 points

Now you can calculate the flow of value by the below formula

Flow of value = velocity / Impediments.

If the current average velocity of the team is say 45 and sum of impediments becomes 25

According to formula Flow of value for the team = 45/25 = 1.8

The flow output indicates the flow efficiency of the team. In this case since the flow output is greater than 1 i.e.1.8 denotes a good flow.

For reference, value flow output > 1 indicates the good flow, on the other hand if the value is < 1 , the team needs immediate attention on impediments over planning for work.

There are 3 types of value

1. Commercial value: How the feature delivered increased the revenue.

2. Future Value: Some features may not fetch immediate revenue but scope to get soon in that case measure future

value which will measure how this feature will save cost or time for the customers?

3. Customer Value: How this feature helps to make customer stay with us and increase the customer base for the product.

If the user stories which can achieve any of the above 3 values are not planned for the sprint, or the user stories with focus of above values are not achieved then 'No value delivered' can be declared.

Building upon this foundational understanding, let's delve into the metrics applicable to diverse units and domains.

Key Inquiries on measurements:

There is always a big questions on what to be measured:

Should we assess Performance? or Optimize Efficiency? or

refine our processes? or

Evaluate Teams?

The Short answer is 'Measure that matters'.

Metrics should be identified based on the areas where improvement is needed within a system, rather than simply adopting metrics used by others. The goal should be clearly defined, and metrics should be tailored to measure the lagging factors to reach the goal.

Identifying and addressing areas for improvement is crucial for continuous progress and achieving desired outcomes. By closely monitoring performance metrics and evaluating current practices, we can pinpoint specific areas that require attention and implement strategies to enhance them. This ongoing process of assessment and refinement ensures that we are consistently moving towards our goals and operating at our highest potential.

Metrics and coaches

Metrics provides indications not solutions.

Metrics and coaches play distinct roles towards improvement. Metrics provide objective data and indications of performance, highlighting areas that need attention. However, they do not offer solutions to the underlying problems.

Coaches, on the other hand, facilitate reflection and exploration, helping individuals and teams identify root causes and develop effective solutions. Through their powerful questioning, coaches empower others to find their own answers. While metrics provide the compass, coaches guide the journey of improvement. Coaches provide reflections not solutions.

<u>Adaptability for metrics:</u>

In our rapidly evolving world, where we operate within an ever-changing environment, can metrics afford to remain rigid and unchanging? Can you identify a metric and keep it static for many years to measure the system? Will they truly serve their intended purpose for any organization?

We absolutely cannot equate any single metric for various teams/ organisation The reason is that the parameters of the system vary rapidly.

Measuring without a clear plan for improvement is an empty exercise that serves no purpose.

<u>Stages of Metrics:</u>

Metrics have three important stages

1. Define your goal.

2. Measure what is lagging.

3. Assess how to improve.

It is important to cite that measuring what is lagging can lead to defining goals too. The earlier approach of defining the goal and measuring is the diagnostic approach of metrics, whereas the later approach of deriving goal from measure is the descriptive approach. Continuous measurement in either way will lead to predictive metrics.

For example, Sprint burndown is a diagnostic approach to track the amount of work done towards the sprint goal.

Measuring Business KPI's may lead to defining the upcoming OKR's which is a Prescriptive approach.

Analysis of cumulative flow diagrams provides insights of throughput which can be described as a predictive approach.

<u>Identify the lagging indicators and map a metric to measure and improve:</u>

Identifying the lagging factors for metrics is an important part of performance analysis and improvement. Lagging factors are the underlying causes or influences that affect a particular metric after the fact. They are often used to understand why a metric performed the way it did and to make data-driven decisions for improvement.

Leading indicators look forwards, through the windshield, at the road ahead. Lagging indicators look backwards, through the rear window, at the road you've already traveled.

Lagging indicators show the indications of happening but don't answer why it happened.

A leader with a coaching mindset in the field can identify the lagging indicators in the system and lead them to the future benefits.

Below tools can be useful to identify the metric to be measured based on the past data called lagging indicators along with strong observational capabilities.

Value Stream Mapping (VSM):

- Description: VSM is a visual representation of a process that helps analyze, optimize, and streamline the flow of materials and information.

- Software Example: Microsoft Visio, Lucidchart, or specialized VSM software like Miro, Mural.

Pareto Chart (80:20 Rule):

- Description: A Pareto Chart displays issues in descending order of importance, making it easy to focus on the most critical factors.

- Software Example: Microsoft Excel, Google Sheets, or dedicated statistical software like Minitab.

Ishikawa Diagram (Cause and Effect):

- **Description:** The Ishikawa Diagram organises potential causes of a problem into categories, helping to identify root causes.

- **Software Example:** Microsoft PowerPoint or specialised diagramming tools like Creately, Miro and Mural.

Kaizen Workshops:

- **Description:** Kaizen workshops require real-time collaboration and can be organized using various project management and collaboration tools.

- **Software Example:** Tools like Trello, Asana, or project management software such as Jira can be used to manage Kaizen workshops.

- **5 Whys:**

- **Description:** The 5 Whys technique can be applied using any text editor or problem-solving software to document and track each "why" question and its answers.

- **Software Example:** Any text editor or even a simple note-taking app can suffice.

Poka Yoke (Mistake Profiling):

- **Description:** Poka Yoke aims to prevent errors in processes and can be integrated into manufacturing software and automation systems.

- **Software Example:** Manufacturing execution systems (MES) and automation software often include Poka Yoke features.

Key Performance Indicator (KPI) Analysis:

- **Description:** KPIs can be tracked and analyzed using various business intelligence and data visualization tools.

- **Software Example:** Tableau, Power BI, Google Data Studio, or custom dashboard solutions.

Visual Management Techniques:

- **Description:** Visual management tools help in real-time tracking and visualization of processes and tasks.

- **Software Example:** Trello, KanbanFlow, Linoit or specialized Lean management software like Kanbanize.

Agile maturity assessment:

- **Description:** An handcrafted customised Agile assessment can provide insights for the team in current Agility levels which may provide insights are lagging factors. Please visit www.agilebodhi.com to download assessment framework and customise for your teams.

Identify org impediment exercise:

Velocity exercise:

- **Description**: This exercise helps identify roadblocks and bottlenecks that hinder the Agile team's velocity

- **How to do:** Create a centralized artifact with each team name and a blank space asking 'What are the inhibitors to deliver the user stories?'. Invite all the agile teams and assign a facilitator for each team.

- Provide a breakout for each team for 2 hour brainstorming to decide the factors of inhibitors.

- Collate the inhibitors which has been provided by many of the teams which becomes the list of Organisational impediment which can be converted as business metric.

- Using the above tools and continuous observation of the system is necessary with Lean and System thinking. Be it team or business, identify the factors which are lagging and focus to improve. Strong suggestion is to identify one lagging metric apart from usual tracking business metrics and improve in a time period. Once it's improved, take up the next metric iteratively.

Introducing Metric Backlog

This chapter introduces the concept of Metric backlog and a prioritization technique for this backlog. In the quest for organizational excellence, establishing a metrics backlog emerges as a strategic approach to prioritizing improvement efforts. Just as a product backlog guides product development, a metrics backlog serves as a roadmap for identifying and addressing performance gaps. This backlog can serve as a repository of potential metrics to work on, ensuring that you always have a pool of ideas to draw from Acronym FOCUS

FOCUS:

- **Focused:** Targets specific areas for improvement and impact.

- **Observable:** Easily measured and visualized data.

- **Concise:** Limited number of essential metrics.

- **Upward Trend:** Capable of sustained improvement and progress.

- **Scalable:** Accommodate increased complexity, team size, or project scope without losing their effectiveness.

Prioritizing Metrics Backlog: A Matrix Approach:

This chapter introduces a matrix approach, the I&I Matrix. Organizations can prioritize their metric backlog in a structured manner, ensuring that resources are focused on the metrics with the greatest potential impact.

X axis is the matrix indicating the impact the metrics impose on a system which is categorised as low impact, medium impact and high impact.

Y axis is the timeline to implement like immediate implementation or long term implementation.

The exercise of I&I matrix may result in following categories:

High Impact, Immediate Implementation

Metrics that fall in the high-impact, immediate implementation quadrant should be prioritized as they have a significant impact on the system and can be implemented quickly. These metrics often address critical issues or opportunities for improvement.

Medium Impact, Immediate Implementation

Metrics in the medium-impact, immediate implementation quadrant should be considered next. While their impact is not as substantial as high-impact metrics, they still offer value and can be implemented relatively quickly.

High Impact, Long-Term Implementation

Metrics with a high impact but requiring a longer implementation timeline should be carefully evaluated. Their significant impact justifies their inclusion in the backlog, but their implementation may require more planning and resources.

Medium Impact, Long-Term Implementation

Metrics in the medium-impact, long-term implementation quadrant should be considered for inclusion based on available resources and strategic priorities. While their impact is not as significant as other metrics, they may still offer long-term benefits.

Low Impact Metrics

Metrics with low impact, regardless of implementation timeline, may not provide sufficient value to justify prioritization. However, they should be reviewed periodically to assess their continued relevance.

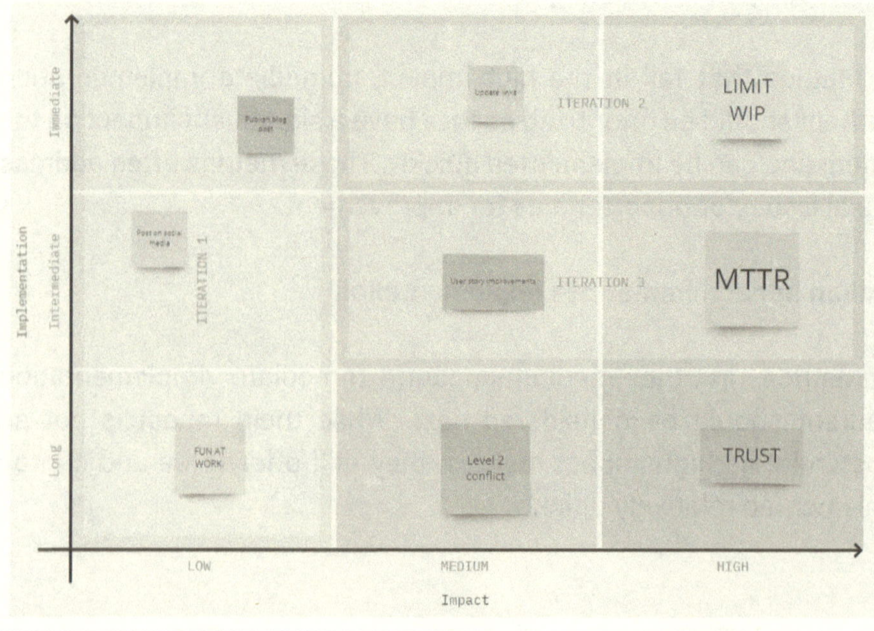

<u>Metrics implementation:</u>

Below is the step by step approach to implement Metrics for Continuous improvement of any unit:

1. **Lean and Systems thinking:** Lean and systems thinking are two complementary approaches that can be used to effectively assess metrics. Lean focuses on minimalistic approach and improving process efficiency, while systems thinking considers the interactions between different parts of a system.

2. **Coaching skills:** A Coach is capable of viewing the system objectively, where focus primarily resides on non judgemental observation before implementation. Powerful questions at this point would stimulate critical thinking, and uncover underlying assumptions.

3. **Root cause Analysis:** By continuously observing the system and processes, deploy the tools like Value stream mapping, ishikawa diagram, pareto analysis with which you can uncover root causes and areas for improvement.

4. **Focus on Lagging Metrics:** Identifying specific lagging metrics that are critical to your goals is a valuable approach. By concentrating your efforts on improving one metric at a time, you can effectively track progress and make meaningful changes.

5. **Metric Backlog:** Creating a metrics backlog for teams, departments, or the entire organization is a structured way to prioritize improvement efforts. Metrics backlog is a single artifact to track and maintain the whole organizations and business metrics.

6. **Prioritization Using Impact and Implement Matrix (I&I):** To prioritize the metric backlog effectively, organizations

can employ an Impact and Implementation (I&I) Matrix. This matrix categorizes metrics based on their impact on the system (low, medium, or high) and their implementation timeline (immediate or long-term).

7. **Customization for Your Purpose:** Tailoring the I&I matrix to your organization's specific needs and objectives is a great way to ensure that the prioritization process aligns with your unique challenges and goals.

8. **Data-Driven Decision-Making:** The use of metrics and data to guide decisions is a fundamental aspect of Lean and System thinking. It encourages evidence-based choices and helps ensure that improvements are well-informed.

9. **Iterative Process:** Keep in mind that the process of improving lagging metrics is iterative. As you work on one metric and see improvements, you can move on to the next, constantly cycling through the process to drive ongoing performance enhancement at least in quarterly cycles.

10. **Communication and Transparency:** Ensure that the process and results of your metric improvement efforts are communicated transparently across your organization. This can help build buy-in and collaboration among teams.

The above market tested approach is aligned with best practices in Agile process improvement and data-driven management. By systematically identifying and addressing lagging metrics, you can create a culture of continuous improvement and enhance the overall performance of your teams or organization.

This is one of the major reasons why we are being particular about "Metrics in IT" in this chapter. Though the word metrics might be common, what we measure, how we measure and when/where we measure varies in the IT industry. Hence list of metrics applicable for teams, organization and business is provided in the further chapters.

Who should measure:

In line with Agile principles of self-organization and empowerment, the measured unit should take ownership of measuring and tracking their own performance metrics. This fosters a sense of accountability and drives continuous improvement.

Organization leaders should be consulted and informed about team metrics to gain insights and provide support, but they should not impose metrics or hold teams directly accountable. Instead, their focus should be on identifying and improving organization-level metrics that align with overall business objectives.

Metrics are not for monitoring, but for continuous improvement.

Metrics implementation can be resistive from teams in IT due to their association with blame rather than improvement. Post-measurement evaluations should focus on fostering a growth mindset.

Similarly, business leaders should measure and enhance business metrics, while relying on team and organization leaders for their respective performance data. This collaborative approach ensures that metrics are used effectively for continuous improvement at all levels, leading to a more agile and successful organization.

Agile and Metrics:

The below picture is the original draft of Agile principles in its birth year 2001. Agile has been founded by 17 software professionals for the IT industry. Fascinatingly, the original authors have classified Agile principles into three primary categories: Customers, Managers, and Teams. Each Agile value and principle is intricately connected to metrics. The deliberate agile and principles which speaks on metrics are

- 7th Working software is the primary measure of progress.

- 9th Continuous attention to technical excellence and good design enhances agility.

- 12th At regular intervals, the team reflects on how to become more effective, then tunes and adjusts its behaviour accordingly.

By an extraordinary coincidence, this book is also structured around these same three major areas: 1. Business, 2. Organization, and 3. Teams. I'm pleased to announce that this book offers metrics for each Agile principle within these three categories, and we will kickstart our exploration with a focus on team.

Principles (Draft as of 4/1/2001)

Our highest priority is to satisfy the customer through early and continuous delivery of valuable software.

Welcome changing requirements, even late in development. Agile processes harness change for the customer's competitive advantage.

Deliver working software frequently, from a couple of weeks to a couple of months, with a preference to the shorter timescale.

Business people and developers must work together daily throughout the project.

Build projects around motivated individuals. Give them the environment and support they need, and trust them to get the job done.

The most efficient and effective method of conveying information to and within a development team is face-to-face conversation.

Working software is the primary measure of progress.

Agile processes promote sustainable development. The sponsors, developers, and users should be able to maintain a constant pace indefinitely.

Continuous attention to technical excellence and good design enhances agility.

Simplicity--the art of maximizing the amount of work *not* done--is essential.

The best architectures, requirements, and designs emerge from self-organizing teams.

At regular intervals, the team reflects on how to become more effective, then tunes and adjusts its behavior accordingly.

Chapter 2

Team Metrics

Art of togetherness is core of Agile

- Padma

In the knowledge-driven terrain of software development, the exchange of experiences and ideas is paramount for both individual and organizational growth.

Agile methodologies advocate for team-based approaches, recognizing that collaboration, trust, and respect are cornerstones of successful software delivery. While individual contributors can make significant contributions, Agile teams leverage the following to deliver high-quality software products that adapt to evolving needs.

- collective intelligence,

- cross-functional expertise,

- rapid feedback,

- shared ownership,

- and enhanced morale to deliver

Agile is an iterative and incremental approach which paves the way for a rhythmic and repeated stop-watch-learn-continue-improve approach which makes metrics as a continuous process rather than a quarterly/yearly review.

Team Maturity vs Metrics:

Software teams represent the driving force behind transformative ideas and valuable software solutions. However, the effectiveness of the teams is not static; it evolves over time, influenced by factors such as individual growth, project complexity, and organizational culture. To effectively measure and improve the performance of software teams, it is crucial to tailor metrics to the team's current maturity level.

The maturity of an Agile team is determined by its ability to operate as a self-organizing unit. As an Agile team matures, its metrics need to be revisited and refined to reflect its evolving capabilities and focus.

<u>Pragmatic approach for team metrics based on their maturity:</u>

There are many maturity models available for agile teams assessment. Now, let's discuss the team metrics with the well known Shu Ha Ri team maturity model.

The Shu-Ha-Ri model provides a valuable framework for guiding agile teams on their journey towards maturity. It emphasizes the importance of starting with a strong foundation in the core principles of agility, followed by a period of experimentation and adaptation, ultimately leading to a level of mastery where teams can innovate and thrive in an ever-changing environment.

Shu (Adherence)

In the Shu stage of agile team maturity, teams focus on following established agile practices and methodologies. They adopt the prescribed rituals and ceremonies, such as daily stand-ups, sprint planning, and retrospectives, without fully understanding the underlying principles. This stage is crucial for establishing a consistent rhythm of work and building a foundation of shared understanding.

Ha (Adaptability)

As teams gain experience and familiarity with agile practices, they transition into the Ha stage. They begin to question and adapt the prescribed practices to better suit their specific context and challenges. They experiment with different techniques and approaches, learning from their successes and failures. This stage fosters innovation and continuous improvement.

Ri (Mastery)

Reaching the Ri stage of agile team maturity signifies a deep understanding of agile principles and a high degree of adaptability. Teams have internalized the essence of agility and can seamlessly apply it to their work. They can self-organize, manage dependencies, and continuously adapt to changing circumstances. They have become true masters of agile practices.

<u>Best practice of software metrics for newly formed 'Shu' Agile teams:</u>

Launch a team with fixed iteration and fixed team members. This enables us to keep a stable platform with which we can accommodate the dynamic parameter called 'Scope'. Change in scope is inevitable in the IT industry. Hence keeping a static team and iteration can be considered a prudent approach.

Frequent switching between projects can lead to chaos and make it difficult to measure past performance and estimate future scope.

In an agile setup, people movement between projects is kept minimal for following reasons:

- **Cohesion and productivity:**

   When team members are constantly moving to different projects, it can take time for them to learn the new project, build relationships with their new team members. This can disrupt the team's workflow and lead to decreased value flow.

- **Familiar With the project's domain and requirements:**

  When team members have a deep understanding of the project's domain and requirements, they are better able to make informed decisions and deliver high-quality work.

- **Context switching:**

  Moving team members to new projects too frequently can increase the amount of transitioning from one task to another which can lead to decreased value flow and increased errors. It is worthy to comment that context switching also applies to changing scope and task which may also lead to the above cited implications.

- **Velocity Impact:**

  Velocity is the rate at which a team can deliver completed work. When team members are constantly moving to different projects, it can disrupt the team's velocity and make it difficult to predict when the project will be completed. Predictability in team velocity will lead to insights, valuable for upcoming sprints and estimating the team's capacity for future work.

- **Knowledge Continuity:**

  When team members move to new projects, they take their knowledge with them. This can lead to a loss of knowledge within the team making it difficult for continuous value flow. Identifying opportunities to reduce single person dependency and frequent cross learning might reduce the impact.

In some cases, it may be necessary to move team members to different projects. However, this should be done on a case-by-case basis only when it is absolutely necessary.

As a next step, Customise the agile framework for the team.

There are various Agile frameworks (e.g., Scrum, Kanban, XP and Scaling frameworks). Choose or combine frameworks that align with the team's goals and constraints.

As a further step define the relative estimation technique to the teams,

Why Relative Estimates?

Relative estimates are also more flexible than absolute.

Relative estimates are a flexible way to estimate the effort required to complete a software development project apart from the benefits like improved transparency, collaboration.

T-shirt sizing is usually deployed to size complex scope such as features and EPICS. Fibonacci sequence can be more relevant for granular user stories.

Most applied and proven useful for Shu teams are planning poker based fibonacci series estimation for each user story. Sum the estimation of completed user stories adhering with DOD(Definition of Done) becomes velocity.

Estimation by the Doers

Please remember that this estimation should be done by the professionals who are involved in execution of work. This is because the team members have the best understanding of the project requirements and the technical complexity of each user story. In a case where the team requires additional understanding and seek support, they still remain the appropriate party to provide the estimate as executioners of the commitment. They are also able to consider their own capacity and availability when making. There is a trend where the team member who is assigned to complete a user story estimates for the user story which should be avoided. Please note that estimation should be done as a team not as an individual.

<u>Do not convert story points to hours/days:</u>

Converting relative estimates to hours is a common pitfall for organizations and teams. This should be strictly avoided, as it undermines the logic of empirical relative agile estimation.

First let's understand the concept of story points from its ideator Ron. In the words of Ron Jeffries:

We multiplied Ideal Days by a "load factor" to convert to actual implementation time. Load factor tended to be about three: three real days to get an Ideal Day's work done. We spoke of our estimates in days, usually leaving "ideal" out. The result was that our stakeholders were often confused by how it could keep taking three days to get a day's work done, or, looking at the other side of the coin, why we couldn't do 50 "days" of work in three weeks. So, as I recall it, we started calling our "ideal days" just "points". And we really only used the points to decide how much work to take into an iteration anyway, so if we said it was about 20 points, no one really objected".

Though the above statement provides a background on how story points came to be, please note that its based on the principle: It is often easier to compare the size of one task with another, rather than trying to assign an exact numerical value.

However, it's important to note that story points are relative to specific Agile teams, and the same story might have a different number of story points in different teams. This is because it's a measure of perceived effort, ambiguity and complexity, not an absolute metric.

While it is possible to quantify effort in terms of numerical values like days or hours, it is more challenging to quantify ambiguity and complexity, as these are subjective qualities that depend on various factors. However, story points though not assigning a value for ambiguity and complexity it helps to indicate the size of the ambiguity and complexity presence. Hence this book strongly advocates not to convert story points into days/hours.

Many interpret velocity as a metric but it's more of a data from which powerful measurements can be made for agile teams.

For example, Predictability, completion rate, Sprint addition rate etc.,

Predictability is the percentage of story points that were committed to a sprint and completed during that sprint

Addition rate: The ratio of story points that were added to an active sprint /story points committed during sprint planning /sprint start.

Completion rate: Percentage of added and committed story points that were completed out of the total committed story points for all completed sprints

To start with metrics for shu team, its ideal to start with sprint predictability as a metric,

Predictability % = Completed story points/ Committed story points *100

Based on the inference from various research teams, output < 80% or higher completed vs committed percentage indicates teams commitment to produce good value flow. However, the output range should be consistent to conclude that the team is predictable.

If the team's score is anything less than 80%, the root cause of the team's instability should be investigated. An agile coach/scrum master can partner with leaders to identify the gap and address the root cause of the commitment deviation.

This book suggest not to intervene the sprint backlog once sprint starts and revision or providing story points after sprint start is not advised. Formulas which includes such parameters of calculation is not discussed in the book to discourage such practices and formulas. However due to unavoidable circumstances if any work item is added to a sprint, its good to measure the sprint completion rate over sprint predictability.

Sprint completion rate = (Initially committed and completed story points + Included and completed story points)/Initially commited story points. This percentage can be more than 100% at times.

Metric for Product backlog for Shu team is Backlog health - It denotes the Story readiness for upcoming sprints. N+1 story readiness is mandatory. N+2 is advisable. N+3 and above are not realistic and as a matter of fact It's anti-agile.

As teams embark on their Agile journey, the Shu stage signifies a crucial phase of establishing a solid foundation for collaboration and process adherence. Metrics in this stage play a pivotal role in assessing the team's grasp of Agile fundamentals and their ability to follow established practices.

Technical Skills and Knowledge:

- Agile Training Completion: Measures the team's exposure to Agile principles and practices.

- Agile Concept Explanation: Assesses the team's ability to articulate and apply Agile concepts.

- Agile Best Practice Identification: Evaluates the team's capacity to recognize and implement effective Agile practices.

Process Adoption and Adherence:

- Agile Ceremony Compliance: Measures the team's adherence to Agile rituals, such as daily stand-ups, retrospectives, and planning meetings.

- User Story Quality: Assesses the team's ability to create clear and actionable user stories. User stories should be vertical slicing over horizontal slicing.

Collaboration and Communication:

- Meeting Participation: Measures the team's engagement and contribution during meetings.

- Open Communication: Assesses the team's ability to foster open and honest communication.

- Collaboration Satisfaction: Evaluates the team's overall perception of collaboration and teamwork.

By monitoring these metrics, Shu maturity teams can identify areas for improvement and ensure that they are building a strong foundation for their Agile journey.

Best practices of metrics for 'Ha' agile team:

HA team indicators are

1. Predictability score is healthy.

2. Relationships between team members are flourishing.

3. Team exhibits cross functional skills.

Now it's time to enhance the team from the current state of metrics.

Velocity at this stage remains a point of reference to measure teams maturity.

So what should be done?

Cycle time should be measured and improved upon.

How?

At this point, the team should begin cross-functional work, where any team member is willing to take on any task, even if they are not yet proficient in the additional skills.

Now in Daily stand up meeting, few things Ha maturity team should do are:

1. Discuss the WORK ITEM AGE.

2. Check the WIP limit.

Cycle Time — the amount of elapsed time between when a work item starts and when a work item finishes.

Work Item Age — the amount of time between when a work item started and the current time.

Now based on Work item age, team members should decide which product backlog item is best to work upon. They may put a pause on the item which they are currently working on and replan to work on the item with a high work item age. Please note that work item age and cycle time are considered inside the sprint window.

In this way, the team reduces the cycle time of user stories which is a more efficient indicator of the team.

At the end of the sprint, the cycle time of each user story can be measured and averaged, which would ideally be better than the previous sprint. This approach is tried and tested in many agile teams and proven useful.

Limit WIP.

Moving away from working in silos to a collaborative environment leads to enhanced value flow.

10 people working on 3 user stories and completing 100% with 2 more stories yet to begin is more valuable than working on 5 user stories and completing 50% of work in a sprint.

Ha team benefits from utilising work item age accountability, as part of cycle time.

In this way, measuring cadence is reduced from per sprints to per day.

Beyond Estimates - Unleashing the Power of Measurement in Agile Projects

Predictive systems, often employed in industries like finance and healthcare, utilize historical data and statistical models to forecast future trends and patterns. This approach proves valuable in situations where analyzing current conditions provides sufficient information to predict future outcomes.

In contrast, volatile systems, prevalent in the IT domain, exhibit a high degree of uncertainty and unpredictability. Rapid technological advancements, shifting market demands, and evolving user preferences render estimations less reliable in such environments.

In Agile project management, leaning on the metrics, beyond estimates is generally more reliable for gauging progress and making informed decisions.

Best practices for 'Ri' team:

By the time the team reaches Ri stage, a lot of improvements in technical and psychological aspects can be observed.

Indicators of Ri team:

- Cross functional transformation.

- Psychological safety.

What should be measured:

At this stage, metrics will be defined, measured and improved by the team. No external support is needed. Allow them to break the rules and innovate by themselves and build a Metric backlog for the team.

Metrics backlog serves a strong self-organized accountability for improvement. For details on creating and implementing Metrics backlog refer back to chapter 1.

Measure the value delivery. Formula cited in chapter 1 to measure value delivery can be applied and evaluated periodically.

At this stage, it's more we vs I not only between team members but with all other agents. It should be a collaborative effort b/w business and tech team. They should open up with happenings on both sides and ideate, brainstorm and build the next level of product/service.

Once the Ri stage is realised, it is vital to understand the center point of progress hereafter. This is the driving force behind ensuring an iterative cycle for the team.

Kokoro: The Heart of Mastery

Kokoro is the advanced stage of the Shu Ha Ri learning model. It is the stage of mastery, where the practitioner has not only learned the rules and techniques of their art, but has also developed a deep understanding of the underlying principles. At this stage, the practitioner is able to transcend the rules and create their own unique style.

Kokoro is often described as a state of "flow," where the practitioner is completely absorbed in their activity and feels as if they are one with their art. They are no longer thinking about the rules or techniques, but are simply responding to the situation in an intuitive and natural way.

In the context of agile, Kokoro is the stage where teams have developed a deep understanding of agile principles and practices. They are able to apply these principles and practices to their work in a way that is both effective and efficient. They are also able to adapt their approach to different situations and challenges.

At the Kokoro stage, the relationships are stronger and trustworthy. Learning opportunities are considered a growth for the individuals and teams. Here, Metrics is not a formal activity but an everyday improvement.

The metrics described above are a common and useful set of essential metrics for teams. In subsequent pages, an overview of the metrics that agile teams can track based on lagging factors are presented.

Common dysfunctions of Software teams on Metrics:

Parallel execution of user stories:

One person- one story approach in user stories execution is one of common dysfunction. There is a usual tendency of team members to take each one story for execution which may lead to non-completion of value production. Best practice is to determine a WIP limit for every team and verify this limit being sustained through daily check-points.

Irrespective of the teams maturity the intervention to team backlog after sprint start should be discouraged. In other words Sprint addition rate should be ideally zero to keep velocity in good track. Sprint addition rate = Added points/initally committed points *100

Lack of Test Automation

There has been a remarkable increase in the test automation focus over the last decade. However, the frequency of BDD based test suits being executed has been limited. A focused discussion on this aspect across the team during the daily check-points can lead to encouragement of each user story integration, inline increasing the quality and value of the product.

Shift-left initiatives by organisations which are trending currently is a practice that involves moving testing, quality, and performance evaluation earlier in the development process, often before any code is written.

Shift left enables all the team members irrespective of skills to take accountability of quality.

3. Story Slicing

In general, vertical slicing is the preferred approach for breaking down user stories in agile projects. However, the manner in which these user stories are decomposed can significantly impact the project's overall success. A common mistake observed in the Agile ways of working is the tendency to slice user stories horizontally rather than vertically. Horizontal slicing as much as it seems easy on the eyes, it does reap the benefits of being agile. Along side enough detailed acceptance criteria are crucial for teams value flow.

Metrics tracking

As with all the dysfunctions discussed up until now, there is a keen emphasis on checking-in with the team daily. Reiterating the same across all aspects of work through a metric will only ensure transparency and collaboration across the team. This feeds into the need for feedback, which also acts as a metric.

Velocity comparison across teams

Having seen the origin of velocity as its sum of relative story points, comparing different teams' velocities may seem illogical. A team usually settles into a velocity organically based on context, skill and capacity. With humans bringing their most unique personalities to their teams, comparison across teams may lead to comparing apples and oranges.

Review meetings aren't exams

Review meetings are the window for Users and stakeholders how their thought/ idea has conceptualized into a working component. At the same time the team is eager to showcase what they have developed from the received requirements. Feedback here can be provided from either way.

Technical metrics as an option

Review meetings demonstrate the work accomplished to stakeholders. This book recommends reviewing technical metrics at this point, where tools like JaCoCo, Cobertura and Emma can be utilised. Additionally, code coverage and static code analysis can be analysed using tools like Sonar cube.

Retrospective - ticking the box

Inspect and adapt is the nerve of scrum events.

When "ideas for a retrospective" is brought up, it is usually taken up as a mandate to action upon or a box to tick off the ceremonies.

However, individuals opening up to provide/receive feedback in such environments is not proven successful. Here the recommendation for the facilitator is to approach a Retrospective with a Coaching mindset where thought-provoking ideas and feedback are exchanged.

i. Process over people

When a team has visual differences across the team, the need for adding a process to ease the environment and "get the job done" has been a trend across many transformations. The innate ability to address the individual differences is sidelined. In hindsight, a process is added to the system where people's issues need addressing.

As long as humans are operating software systems, there is a need to address the people's side of agility.

Apart from the quantitative measures, the below should be a primary metric measured in regular cadence.

Do I feel like I belong to the team?

Do I feel good expressing my opinion?

Do I enjoy the company of team members?

Was it individual or team work?

No of defects are not to be judged

No. of defects is an usual metric followed by a team but it's not a very useful measure. Try not to judge the team based on high/low defects. Rather encourage the team to look into open defects, leaked defects and defects resolution time.

Unhealthy Builds

Build health is a crucial metric that reflects the overall quality and stability of a software development process. A successful build run indicates that the code has passed all compilation, testing, and packaging steps without encountering any errors or issues. Build health can be one of the dicussion in review meeting.

Velocity Target

Common comment of leaders for the teams is 'Increase your velocity by 10% in next quarter'.

It doesn't needs a quarter to increase velocity rather just a sprint. But thats not real development. Decrease the cycle time rather than increasing velocity of teams.

Performance Evaluation through Velocity

The most common metric an agile team is said to track is Velocity.

However, Velocity is not a metric, rather it's data that is not a direct measure of team performance, but can be used to track progress over time and forecast future work.

Ignoring Cumulative flow diagram

'Cumulative flow diagram (CFD) is often underrated report by agile practitioners. However, this is the place where bottlenecks can be identified.

Process bottlenecks are factors which slow down the flow of a system.

The ability to show bottlenecks in the development process is the key advantage of cumulative flow diagrams over burn up charts.

Metrics through Reports:

All agilists lean towards wanting a visual representation of the work accomplished. Are the same individuals mindful of what these reports represent? What are the inputs and when is the right time to use which report?

Chart	What	Why	When
Velocity chart	Tracks the average amount of work completed per unit of time.	To understand a team's capacity and make predictions about future work.	At the end of each sprint or iteration.
Cumulative flow diagram	Visualizes the workflow of a process and identifies bottlenecks.	To understand how work is flowing through a process and identify areas for improvement.	At regular intervals, such as daily or weekly.
Burndown chart	Shows the amount of work remaining in a project over time.	To track progress towards a project goal and identify potential problems.	Daily or weekly, depending on the length of the project.
Burnup chart	Shows the amount of work completed in a project over time.	To track progress towards a project goal and visualize the overall scope of the project.	Daily or weekly, depending on the length of the project.
Control charts	Monitor processes to detect and eliminate variation.	To identify and eliminate sources of variation in a process, such as defects	As part of a continuous improvement process.

Individual metrics:

Individuals with skills are the primary resource for any IT organisation and value is delivered by groups of these individuals - Teams. The temptation for organisations to solely drive individual productivity, contradicts the concept of "team progress".

Is tracking individual productivity a viable metric?

Can this be quantitatively measured by the number of lines of code, test cases accomplished or bug found? Not Quite.

An organisations' performance evaluation includes relative comparisons between team members. So, does it mean that individuals in IT organisation are not entitled for measurement?

No

As suggested in this book already, every entity in the system is entitled for metrics.

In this case, the measurement cannot be limited for an appraisal cycle.

The change proposed:

Individuals should measure themselves for Continuous improvement and not only for appraisals. Here's what is to be measured:

- Focus time

- organisation goal alignment

- Learning

Metrics that focus on qualitative measurement are known as "soft" metrics. Unlike hard metrics, which focus on objective and measurable data, soft metrics use subjective data and interactive responses to determine an employee's effectiveness. Soft metrics stress the impact that human capital has on business outcomes.

Collaborative compatibility is a primary factor in team success, beyond technical skills.

Create a Metrics backlog with both quantitative and qualitative metrics.

Qualitative and quantitative metrics both play a crucial role in evaluating and optimizing various aspects of a team. While quantitative metrics provide measurable and objective data, qualitative metrics offer deeper insights into factors like Happiness index, intrinsic motivations. A Coaching mindset is much needed to understand and gauge the qualitative metrics.

Happiness Index

As metrics are explored in this book, it would make sense to track happiness of individuals and teams as a metric as well. Would it be as linear as an Employee Satisfaction survey? Not quite. This is because satisfaction does not always imply happiness as well.

You cannot be happy at work if you are not satisfied. The vice-versa is not true.

By now, it is clear that humans are the differentiating factor in any organisation and standardising a soft metric can be misleading to individual strengths. So, maintaining a standard in this regard is a challenge.

However, a Happiness Index can be observed of how people feel at work.

Happiness is a state of mind, an emotion, which is beyond monetary rewards and promotions. This state of mind includes an individuals' positivity, trust, job satisfaction, team rapport and primarily leads to Intrinsic motivation.

In today's dynamic and competitive business landscape, employee happiness has emerged as a crucial factor in organizational success. Recognizing the profound impact of a happy and engaged workforce, the concept of the Employee Happiness Quotient (EHQ) has gained significant traction. Pioneered by Raymond D. Zinn, author of the insightful book "Tough Things First," the EHQ provides a simple yet effective framework for assessing and enhancing employee well-being within an organization.

Decoding the EHQ Formula

The EHQ formula, as proposed by Zinn, involves evaluating four key dimensions that contribute to employee happiness:

1. Employee Recognition: Measuring the extent to which employees feel valued and appreciated for their contributions.

2. Supervisors: Assessing the quality of leadership and support provided by managers.

3. The Work: Evaluating the overall satisfaction with job roles, responsibilities, and opportunities for growth.

4. The Company: Gauging the level of engagement and alignment with the organization's mission, values, and culture. **REWRITE**

To calculate the EHQ, each dimension is scored on a scale of one to ten, with ten representing the highest level of satisfaction. The overall EHQ is then determined by adding the scores of all four dimensions. A score below 28, according to Zinn, indicates a potential for demotivation and dissatisfaction among employees.

Customisation

Similar to Ray's approach, every organization can devise a formula including elements that make employees happy: recognition, appreciation, clarity on goals, clarity on job role, tools to excel at work, engagement, feedback, skill development, rewards, fun at work, flexibility, growth options to list a few.

Measuring and Tracking Progress

Regularly assessing the EHQ through employee surveys and feedback mechanisms provides valuable insights into the overall level of happiness and satisfaction within the organization. Identifying trends and areas for improvement allows for continuous optimization of workplace practices and initiatives

Intrinsic motivation is a magic wand that can drive employee engagement, and innovation. When employees are intrinsically motivated, they are driven by a desire to do their work well because they find it challenging, meaningful, and enjoyable. This type of motivation is often more sustainable than extrinsic motivation, which relies on rewards or punishments.

Collective Metric List:

Agile metrics are a valuable tool for helping software teams to measure and improve their performance. However, it is important to choose the right metrics and to use them in a way that is aligned with agile values and principles.

When choosing agile metrics for teams, it is important to consider the specific needs of the team and the project. There is no one-size-fits-all approach to agile metrics. Some common agile metrics for teams include (in no particular order):

Metric	Type	Description	Measurement Frequency
Team morale	Team	How happy and motivated is the team?	Sprint, Release
Customer satisfaction	Team	How satisfied are customers with the product?	Sprint, Release
Technical debt	Team	Technical debt is the cost of additional rework caused by choosing an easy solution now instead of using a better approach that would take longer. How much tech debt does the team owe?	Sprint, Release
Code quality	Team	How well-written and maintainable is the code?	Sprint, Release
Team collaboration	Team	Does the team work well and get along with each other?	Sprint, Release
Process improvement	Team	How well is the team continuously improving their process?	Sprint, Release
Throughput	Team	Number of work items finished per unit of time.	Sprint, Release
Code standard coverage	Team	Percentage of code that compiles to the agreed coding standards	Sprint, Release
Cycle time	Team	Amount of time from the work starts on a release until the point where it is actually released	Sprint, Release
Work item age	Individual, Team	Elapsed time between when a work item started and the current time	Daily, Sprint, Release
Feature test coverage	Team	Percentage of features that is covered in a functional test	Sprint, Release

Work in progress	Team	Number of work items started but not finished (According to DOD)	Daily, Sprint
Build and integration frequency	Team	Number of integrated and tested builds per time period	Daily, Sprint
Defect	Team	Change in defects since last measurement	Sprint, Release
Velocity	Team	Amount of work a team can take during a single sprint	Sprint
Number of defects after release	Team	Leaked defects from development	Sprint, Release
Failed deployment	Team	Number of failed deployments	Sprint, Release
Escaped defects	Team	Number of bugs after release	Sprint, Release
Test automation	Team	Number of automated tests / Total number of tests	Sprint, Release
Days since last user engagement	Continuous	Have this number as minimal as possible for shorter feedback loop. We can save money by not building something with assumptions and corrections.	Daily
Number of experiments	Discrete	Create many spike user story to research the technical spike	Weekly
Flow efficiency	Team	How is current flow of value to customers? What impediments are stopping the flow?	Sprint
Impediments numbers	Discrete	Track the number of impediments that are blocking progress	Weekly

Dependencies nodes between units in organisation	Discrete	Identify and track dependencies between different units in the organization	Quarterly
Action progress from inspect and adapt cycle	Continuous	Measure the progress of actions taken during the inspect and adapt cycle	Monthly
Usable items from customers	Discrete	Measure the number of usable items delivered to customers	Monthly
Happiness Index	Quantitative	A measure of overall well-being and satisfaction with life	Quarterly
Intrinsic Motivation	Qualitative	A measure of the degree to which employees are motivated by internal factors such as interest, challenge, and meaning	Semi-annually

Chapter 3

Organizational Metrics

Excellent firms don't believe in excellence - only in constant improvement and constant change

- Tom peters

Constant improvement and agile are two complementary concepts.

Agile is not fail- proof. But agile enables us to visualize the failures faster with continuous monitoring and improvement.

How?

Measure all the components of the organization continuously in a timeline.

What would happen when measured?

Further clarity on uncertainties are identified and strategies for the future created.

Agile challenges organizations to change as the market evolves, but too much change can also dilute their vision. So, how can organizations be agile without diluting their vision?

A pragmatic approach for an organisation:

1. Set the overall organisation vision.
2. Break down the vision into strategic goals.
3. Launch an initiative to achieve the strategic goals with Minimal risk and maximum benefits.
4. With data, check if strategic goals require adjustment, inline with the vision.

Being an Agile organisation is a mindset to revise the strategic goals as early as possible.

Agile isn't only about completing tasks; it's also about the way tasks are tackled.

Initially, organizational leaders aimed to achieve strategic goals. Actions tracked with respect to strategic goals is a one way, a top-down approach. A suggestion here is to look at a collective approach, measured at each level.

Organizational metrics can be segregated in five major categories:

- **Financial metrics:** Revenue, Profit, return on investment, customer acquisition cost, customer lifetime value, Annual recurring revenue. , revenue per employee.

- **Operational metrics:** Lead time, customer satisfaction, employee turnover, defect rate, on-time delivery, EPIC burndown, Release burndown, control chart, Installed version index, MTTR

- **People metrics:** Employee engagement, training hours, diversity and inclusion metrics, cognitive metrics.

- **Customer metrics:** Net promoter score, customer churn rate, customer satisfaction

- **Innovation metrics:** Number of new products launched, number of patents filed, research and development spending, Innovation rate

- Each of these metrics plays a crucial role in the growth and sustainability of an organisation.

Financial metrics:

Financial metrics are common for organizational metrics which are vital for understanding the financial health of a company and its ability to generate profits. They can be used to measure a company's profitability, efficiency, liquidity, and solvency. Financial metrics can also be used to track a company's progress toward its strategic goals.

- **Revenue:** The Agile approach encourages a flexible response to changing market demands and customer needs, allowing the organization to maximize revenue potential.

- **Profit: By** continuously assessing and adapting to customer feedback, Agile teams can focus on developing features or products that contribute to profitability.

- **Return on Investment (ROI):** Agile principles align well with calculating ROI, as Agile teams can adjust their strategies and priorities based on emerging data and customer feedback.

- **Customer Acquisition Cost (CAC):** Iteratively refining marketing and sales efforts based on customer insights and feedback leads to lower CAC.

- **Customer Lifetime Value (CLV):** By continuously improving the customer experience and aligning products with customer needs, they can enhance CLV.

- **Annual Recurring Revenue (ARR):** ARR is a key financial metric for subscription models, and Agile enables organizations to evolve incrementally and maintain these revenue streams effectively.

- **Revenue Per Employee:** Cross-functional teams, self-organization, and iterative development all contribute to the efficient utilization of human resources, thus potentially increasing revenue per employee.

Dynamic budgeting:

- Traditional budgeting practices often involve fixed annual plans, but dynamic budgeting offers a more flexible approach.

- Dynamic budgeting is well-suited for agile organizations that can quickly adapt to changing circumstances. Dynamic budgeting fosters responsiveness and decision-making agility, where financial planning aligns with the dynamic nature of agile organizations.

- By choosing dynamic budgeting, organizations can enhance their overall financial performance. Spotify, Amazon, and Netflix are among the companies that have embraced dynamic budgeting.

- Dynamic budgeting enables organizations to adjust their budgets as business conditions and priorities evolve. This adaptability is crucial for agile organizations to maintain a competitive edge.

Incorporating Agile principles into financial management and decision-making processes can lead to dynamic and responsive outcomes such as customer collaboration, flexibility, and iterative improvements. Businesses can better adapt to changing market conditions, enhance customer satisfaction, and ultimately achieve greater financial success.

Operational Metrics:

For making crucial decisions, collecting factual data is vital. This is also a driving force behind leaders taking informed decisions. As cited in chapter 2, quantitative metrics are important for data driven operations. Operational metrics are quantitative measures that provide valuable insights into how well an organization is performing and identify areas for improvement.

- **EPIC Lead time:**

  Cycle Time = Time taken by the team to complete the work

  Lead Time = Insights from the point work is received to the time it's delivered.

  To gain a comprehensive understanding of the overall process efficiency, it's essential to measure both cycle time and lead time. By optimizing both cycle time and lead time, organizations can enhance customer satisfaction, reduce costs, and achieve operational excellence.

- **Customer satisfaction:** This can be tracked by an organization for any ongoing/declining product, by collecting customer feedback. This feedback helps to understand the concerns and implement changes to address the same. Some methods such as surveys, CSAT scores, NPS, Customer Effort Score (CES), Social Media Monitoring, Customer Focus Groups can be used to understand the customer satisfaction index.

- **Employee turnover or attrition:** An organization might track employee turnover to identify areas where they can improve the employee experience. For example, if the organization notices that employee turnover is high in a particular department, this is an opportunity to collect data and utilise the same to address concerns across the board.

- **Defect density:** This metric represents the number of defects per unit of code, product, or service. It provides a general indication of the overall defect level in the organization's products. For example, basis the defect density in a particular product, enhanced testing strategies and review processes can be implemented to address the problem.

- **On-time delivery:** An organization might track on-time delivery to ensure that they are meeting their commitments to customers. For example, if the organization notices that on-time delivery is declining for a particular product, they can investigate the root cause and implement changes to address it. As an agile practitioner for over a couple decades, I have noticed the most common spot to fix the delivery issues in agile teams can be rooted in Agile planning and estimation.

- **EPIC burndown:** A chart that shows how much work is remaining in an EPIC over time. EPICs are large, complex pieces of work that are typically broken down into smaller stories and tasks. By tracking the EPIC burndown, agile organisation can ensure that they are making progress towards completing the EPIC and that they are on track to meet their commitments to clients.

- **Release burndown:** A Release can be inclusive of multiple Epics. This is why it is important to track both Epic and Release burndown charts at an organisation level. By tracking the release burndown, agile teams can ensure that they are on track to release the product or service on time and within budget.

- **Control chart:** A statistical process control chart is used to track the stability of a process and identify trends, variations in the process. This helps agile teams to identify and address potential problems early on.

Observing the cluster of issues and input from standard deviation provides the amount of variation in actual data from the rolling average.

Rolling average(RA): For every issue shown on the chart, the RA (at that point in time) is calculated by taking work items, where X issues occur before the fix and Y issues occur after the fix. The average cycle time of X and Y indicates the total exceeding time for fixing that particular work item.

- **Installed version index (IVI):** IVI is the percentage of customers who are using each version of a product or service. This metric is important for agile organizations because it helps to track the adoption of new features and bug fixes. By tracking the IVI, agile organizations can ensure that their customers are using the most up-to-date and secure version of their product.

- **Mean Time to Repair (MTTR):** This is the average amount of time it takes to fix a defect. MTTR is an important metric for agile organizations because it helps them to track the quality of their products and services. By tracking MTTR, agile organizations can identify areas where they can improve workflow for defect fixes.

Here are some specific examples of how agile organizations and teams can use Organisation operation Metrics to improve performance:

<u>Team</u>

- Use EPIC burndowns to identify which stories in an EPIC are taking the longest to complete. The team can then prioritize these stories and make sure that they are staffed with the appropriate resources.

- Use the release burndown to identify which tasks in a release have impediments. The team can then work to remove these roadblocks and ensure that the release is on track.

- Use the control chart to track the number of defects that are found in each sprint. If the team notices that the number of defects is increasing, they can investigate the root cause of the problem and implement changes to address it.

Organisation:

- Use the installed version index to track the adoption of new features. If the organization notices that a new feature is not being adopted by customers, they can investigate the reasons why and make adjustments to the feature or their marketing strategy accordingly.

- Use MTTR as an impressive data to receive new projects from clients.

People Metrics in Agile Organizations:

Agile organizations recognize that people are their most important asset. As per Shruti kulkarni " "

- **Employee engagement:** This metric measures how motivated and engaged employees are with their work. High employee engagement is essential for agile organizations, as it leads to increased productivity, innovation, and customer satisfaction.

- **Training hours:** This metric tracks the number of hours that employees spend learning and development. Agile organizations invest heavily in training their employees, as they know that this is essential for them to stay ahead of the curve in the rapidly changing business world.

- **Diversity and inclusion metrics:** These metrics track the diversity of the workforce and the organization's commitment to inclusion. A variety of demographics play a big role in today's changing world. Here diversity and inclusion are valued because they know that it leads to better decision-making, innovation and creating safe spaces for growth overall.

- **Cognitive metrics:** These metrics track the cognitive abilities of employees, such as problem-solving skills, creativity, and critical thinking. Cognitive skills are essential for success in the complex and ever-changing agile environment.

By tracking and improving people metrics, agile organizations can create a more engaged, skilled, and diverse workforce. This can lead to a number of benefits, including increased productivity, innovation, and customer satisfaction.

Here are some specific examples of how agile organizations can use people metrics to improve their performance:

- Employee engagement surveys can be used to identify areas where they can improve the employee experience. For example, if the organization notices that employee engagement is low in a particular department, an employee focus group can be conducted to understand their concerns and implement changes to address them.

- An agile organization might track training hours to ensure that employees are getting the training they need to be successful. For example, there could be a goal set for employees to complete a certain number of training hours per year.

- The diversity and inclusion metrics are considered a valuable asset in today's world to track. For example, the organization might track the percentage of employees from different underrepresented groups, genders, geographic locations, learning differences etc.

- An agile organization might track cognitive metrics to ensure that employees have the cognitive skills they need to be successful in the agile environment. For example, the organization might track the results of cognitive ability tests or use gamification platforms to assess employee skills.

Customer metrics:

- Customers are the lifeblood of any business. Measuring the engagement of customers to business is the best and shortest way for feedback. Below are the widely deployed customer metrics

- **Net promoter score (NPS):** This metric measures how likely customers are to recommend the company's products to others. A high NPS indicates that customers are satisfied with the company and are likely to continue doing business with it.

- **Customer churn rate:** This metric measures the percentage of customers who stop using the company's products over a given period of time. A low churn rate indicates that customers are satisfied with the company and are likely to continue doing business with it.

- **Customer satisfaction:** This metric measures how satisfied customers are with the company's products. A high customer satisfaction score indicates that customers are happy with the company's offerings.

Here are some specific examples of how agile organizations can use customer metrics to improve their performance:

- NPS surveys can be used to collect feedback from customers and identify areas of improvement. For example, if the organization notices that customers are dissatisfied with a particular feature, they can prioritize fixing/enhancing it.

- An agile organization might track churn rate to identify customer segments that are at risk of churning. The organization can then take steps to retain these customers, such as offering them discounts or loyalty programs.

- Customer satisfaction surveys are used to collect feedback from customers and identify areas where they can improve the quality of their products. For example, if the organization notices that customers are dissatisfied with the customer support services they are receiving, they can invest in training their support team or implement new support channels.

By using customer metrics effectively, agile organizations can create a more loyal customer base which leads to a number of benefits, including increased revenue and market share.

Innovation metrics:

Agile organizations are known for their ability to innovate rapidly and respond to change effectively. This is due in part to their focus on customer feedback, iterative development, and continuous improvement.

The following innovation metrics can be used to track the performance of agile organizations:

- **Number of new products launched:** This metric measures the number of new products or services that the organization has launched in a given period of time. A high number of new products launched indicates that the organization is innovating and bringing new offerings to market at a rapid pace.

- **Number of patents filed:** This metric measures the number of patents that the organization has filed in a given period of time. A high number of patents filed indicates that the organization is generating and protecting new intellectual property.

- **Research and development spending:** This metric measures the amount of money that the organization is investing in research and development. A high research and development spending indicates that the organization is committed to innovation and is investing in the future.

- **Innovation rate:** This metric measures the rate at which innovative ideas are generated and implemented within the organization.

Innovation Rate = Number of new ideas generated / Number of ideas that are implemented.

A high innovation rate indicates that the organization is able to quickly turn ideas into reality.

Organise the organisation around value, not roles!

Traditional organizational structures centered around hierarchical roles are becoming increasingly obsolete. Organizations must adapt to the evolving demands of the market and customers by shifting their focus from rigid roles to value creation. By organizing around value, businesses can foster a responsive, agile and customer-centric approach, leading to enhanced innovation, improved performance, and sustainable growth.

Organizing around value entails aligning the organizational structure with the specific value streams that deliver benefits to customers. This involves identifying the end-to-end processes that create and deliver value, breaking them down into manageable components, and assigning cross-functional teams to each value stream. These teams are empowered to own the entire value stream, from ideation to delivery, ensuring seamless collaboration and accountability.

The transition from role-based to value-based organization requires a fundamental shift in mindset. This mindset is cultivated through the organisation culture, across all levels.

Empirical estimation of scope:

One of the common troubles for IT leaders is to estimate a scope from the client in an empirical approach.

IT orgs are asked for time and cost the moment they receive the scope from the clients.

Taking this issue as a case study, we have conducted research on the best approach to estimate the scope which can be a feature/epic. This approach is the culmination of 10 years of research. It is an innovative way to solve a complex problem of scope estimation in the IT industry.

Below are the steps

Prerequisite: Fixed team and fixed sprint

Step 1: Split the scope into Epics

Step 2: Any person with product expertise can estimate the split epics with a T-shirt sizing approach

Step 3: Match the T-shirt sizing with the Fibonacci series using the following conversion table.

Step 4: Multiply the outcome with 10. This number would be approximately the sum of story points for the epic, after execution.

Conversion table

XS	1
S	2
M	3
L	5

XL	8
XXL	13
XXXL	21

Example:

Let's assume a team, say Team A, is executing their current sprints with an average velocity of 25 story points.

Now, clients are requesting to develop new functionality in the product which is a potentially huge requirement.

According to the above-shared steps:

Split the functionality into epics.

Now estimate the epics with T shirt sizing, say the Epics are estimated as M and XL and XS according to the Product leaders/ Managers.

According to the above conversation table,

The M epic is 3 points, XL is 8 points and XS is 1 points

Now multiply the estimation with X10 which results as 3 x10 = 30; 8x10 =80 and XS is 10;

Summarize the results: 10+30+80 = 220 points

The skills to develop this functionality is with Team A which exhibits the average velocity as 25 story points.

Step 5: Divide the predicted story points / teams average velocity

220 story points/ 25 - 8.8 ~ to 9 sprints

With 8 team members in Team A and Sprints are executed in a 2 weeks cycle, its 10 working days.

No of members in team: 8

Sprint cycle : 2 weeks

Hence 9 * 10 = 90 days

90 days * 8 = 720 work days.

This approach would be a closer and realistic estimate for epics to predict the timelines to complete the development of the epics in both sprints and man days.

The above method is applicable only when teams are fixed. Also the factor of *10 could vary for orgs. By continuous monitoring of EPICS estimation it may enhance the multiplying factor for more accurate estimates.A sample of Epic tracker provided below:

Name of EPIC	T shirt sizing	Fibbonacci conversated initial story points	Total sprints taken	Actual story points	Lead time of Epic	Teams velocity

Leadership metrics:

How can you measure a leader?

Leadership goals can be measured using quantitative metrics like KPI's and targets but leadership quality is a consistent process to enable others with a growth and open mindset.

Leaders doesn't mean 20 years of experience in senior roles, it can be any title yet the qualities of leadership matters

Self evaluation is the key. As per HUMBLE agile approach proposed by Shruthi kulkarni 'There has been a considerable amount of emphasis on Leaders possessing strong moral values, commitment towards having an Agile mindset and driving change. While Agile "experts" and "Leaders" are expected to truly possess the advantageous Growth Mindset, every individual on the Agile journey will benefit from practising corresponding behaviours, considering the promotion of self-managing and disciplined teams. Leaders can do all that's possible to pave the path, but it's also up-to the individuals to play their role. Agile is now not only about having the mindset anymore. It's also about having the traits that can support this mindset and lead to personal & professional agility.

Each person is a leader, irrespective of the titles held. As agile team members, the influence one has is beyond one team.

Our behaviour and personal characteristics combined is what leads us to building better teams. The Agile Manifesto mentions aspects that one needs to do in order to make Agility successful. What it does not specify is what an individual needs to be to ensure their actions and thoughts can lead them to being Agile.

The HUMBLE Agile approach suggested evaluation and self-awareness across 6 traits, practised on the foundation of Kindness & Compassion.

HUMBLE traits:

Honesty

Unbiased

Mindful

Brave

Listen

Empathy

Evidence Based Management & Organisational metrics

When it comes to organizational agility, one cannot bypass EBM, which is a well composed ready made template to measure organisational agility. EBM indicates the metrics around innovations and value. There are many other categories of measurement for organisational growth like People Metrics and Financial Metrics. Suggestion is to consider the excellent EBM as a framework and customise and top with the additional metrics to derive the metrics backlog for the organisation with which overall metrics being measured.

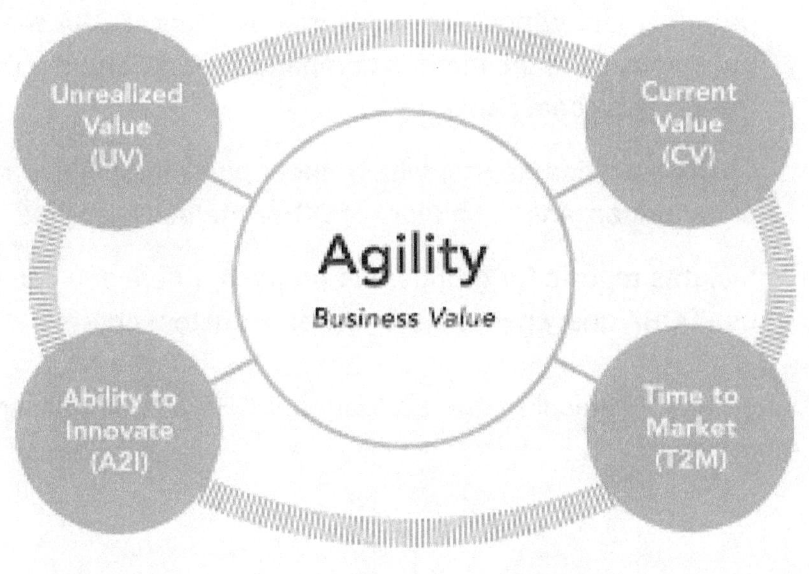

DevOps Research and Assessment (DORA)

Dora

Measuring DevOps maturity of an organisation using DORA metrics serves the purpose. DORA includes four key metrics, divided into two core areas of DevOps:

- Deployment frequency and Lead time for changes measure team velocity.

- Change failure rate and Time to restore service measure stability.

Tracking DORA metrics in Git provides a comprehensive and real-time view of team performance, empowering teams to identify and address bottlenecks, improve their software delivery process, and achieve high-performing DevOps. Relevant to the context of organisation metrics, here are few pointers on DORA to remember:

- Value Streams Dashboard, which helps you identify trends, patterns, and opportunities for improvement. DORA metrics are displayed in the metrics comparison panel and the DORA Performers score panel.

- CI/CD analytics charts, which show pipeline success rates and duration, and the history of DORA metrics over time.

- Insights reports for groups and projects, where you can also use DORA query parameters to create custom charts.

During any technical metric evaluation, DORA can be utilised for maximum benefit.

Organisational metrics backlog

Agile transformation should extend beyond software development teams to encompass the entire organization, fostering a culture of continuous improvement and adaptability. This holistic adoption requires continuous measurement and observation of a comprehensive set of metrics, encompassing financial, people, operational, and innovation aspects.

Metrics backlog is a comprehensive list of metrics that an organization should maintain to track its progress and identify areas for improvement.

The metrics backlog should be reviewed and updated regularly to ensure that it is still relevant to the organization's goals and objectives. The metrics should be tracked and reported on a regular basis to stakeholders so that they can see the organization's progress. The metrics should also be used to identify areas for improvement and to develop corrective actions.

Here is the list of organisation metrics in tabular format:

Category	Metrics	Description
Financial Metrics	Revenue	The total income generated by the business from the sale of goods or services over a specific period.
	Profit	The amount left over after subtracting expenses from revenue, indicating the financial success of the business.
	Return on Investment (ROI)	A measure of the profitability of an investment, calculated as a percentage of the initial investment's gain or loss.

	Customer Acquisition Cost (CAC)	The cost incurred to acquire a new customer, typically calculated by dividing marketing and sales expenses by the number of new customers.
	Customer Lifetime Value (CLV)	The predicted total value a customer will bring to the business throughout their relationship with the company.
	Annual Recurring Revenue (ARR)	The annual income generated from subscription-based or recurring revenue sources.
	Revenue Per Employee	The total revenue divided by the number of employees, indicating the efficiency of the workforce in generating revenue.
Operational Metrics	Lead Time	The time it takes to complete a specific process, from initiation to completion.
	Customer Satisfaction	A measure of how content or dissatisfied customers are with the company's products or services.
	Employee Turnover	The rate at which employees leave the company, often calculated as a percentage of the total workforce.
	Defect Rate	The percentage of defective or faulty products or services produced within a given timeframe.
	On-Time Delivery	The percentage of orders or projects delivered to customers on or before the promised delivery date.
	EPIC Burndown	A visual chart showing the progress of work on a project, specifically for Agile or Scrum methodologies.
	Release Burndown	A chart tracking the completion of tasks or user stories within a release or sprint in Agile development.

	Control Chart	A statistical tool to monitor and control a process's stability and performance over time.
	Installed Version Index	A metric measuring the distribution of different software versions among users or devices.
	Mean Time to Repair (MTTR)	The average time it takes to repair or restore a system or equipment after a failure or issue.
People Metrics	Employee Engagement	A measure of how committed and emotionally connected employees are to their work and the organization.
	Training Hours	The number of hours employees spend in training and development programs.
	Diversity and Inclusion Metrics	Various measures and metrics assessing the organization's commitment to diversity and inclusion in the workplace.
	Cognitive Metrics	Metrics related to the cognitive abilities and performance of individuals, often used in cognitive testing or assessments.
Customer Metrics	Net Promoter Score (NPS)	A metric assessing customer loyalty by asking, "How likely are you to recommend our company to a friend or colleague?"
	Customer Churn Rate	The rate at which customers stop using a product or service, often calculated as a percentage of the customer base.
	Customer Satisfaction	A measure of how pleased or dissatisfied customers are with their experiences with a company's products or services.
Innovation Metrics	Number of New Products Launched	The count of new products or services introduced to the market within a specific time frame.

	Number of Patents Filed	The number of patents for inventions or intellectual property filed by the company.
	Research and Development Spending	The financial investment in research and development activities to create new products, services, or improve existing ones.
	Innovation Rate	A metric reflecting the rate at which innovative ideas are generated and implemented within the organization

Chapter 4

Business Metrics

At Team level metrics - Measure flow

At Organisational metrics - Measure Flow + output

At Business metrics - Measure Flow + output + outcome

Conventional financial and accounting metrics' do not align with the agility required by modern businesses. Such businesses are commonly evaluated using financial metrics such as sales revenue, net profit margin, gross margin, and MRR.

Along with financial measures, is it commonly said that one must measure 'value'. However, how can this value be measured at a business level?

Value réalisation for a Product company could be no of units sold whereas for a Service based business it could be no of customers served. Product-based companies and service-based companies should track the metrics that are most relevant to their specific business models.

Here are a few instances of distinctive metrics for companies and how they are calculated in product-based:

- **Unit economics:** This metric measures the profitability of each unit sold.

- Unit Metric = (Revenue generated by each Unit) - (Cost of goods sold)

- **Product lifetime value (LTV):** This metric measures the total revenue that a customer is expected to generate over the course of their relationship with the company.

- LTV = Average Customer Lifetime x Average Customer Revenue

- **Customer acquisition cost (CAC):** This metric measures the cost of acquiring a new customer.

- CAC = Total marketing and sales costs/ number of new customers acquired.

- **Churn rate:** This metric measures the percentage of customers who stop using the company's product or service over a given period of time.

- **Net promoter score (NPS):** This metric measures customer satisfaction and loyalty. It is calculated by asking customers how likely they are to recommend the product or service to a friend or colleague.

Here are some examples of unique metrics for service-based companies:

- **Utilisation rate:** This metric measures the percentage of time that employees are working on billable projects.

- Utilisation Rate = (total number of hours worked on billable projects) / (total number of hours available)

- **Realisation rate:** This metric measures the percentage of revenue that is actually collected from customers.

- Realisation rate = total revenue collected / total revenue billed.

- **Client satisfaction:** This metric measures how satisfied clients are with the services they have received. It is typically measured through surveys or interviews.

- **Project profitability:** This metric measures the profitability of individual projects.

- Project Profitability = (Revenue generated by the project) - (cost of delivering the project from the revenue)

- **Employee engagement:** This metric measures how engaged employees are with their work and the company. It is typically measured through surveys or interviews.

Though business survival and growth are based on the financial figures and can be a primary measure, it cannot be the only area of focus. Let us explore.

The purpose of a business is to organise some sort of economic production of goods or services.

Businesses can be both profit or non-profit organisations and goals for both differ substantially, the details of which this book does not dive into. Assuming the difference is known, goals of the business drives what an organisation measures.

For any profit based organisations the goals keep revising based on the needs and trends. In a certain year, the goal of the business could be branding over revenue.

There are two important factors of business agility:

1. Looking at the overall business outcome.

2. Compartmentalization of various departments/functions and measure of each unit.

To sail towards our ambitious business goals, we need both a guiding star and a well-oiled engine. Objectives and key results (OKR) are an effective goal setting tool to communicate the business goals to teams. OKRs act as the guiding star, illuminating the distant horizon and aligning everyone's gaze towards that shared destination.

Meanwhile, Key performance indicators (KPI) is a quantifiable measure of performance of various departments/roles in an organisation. KPIs act as the much needed engine, with each team meticulously tracking their unique contributions.

This compartmentalization ensures individual accountability while maintaining focus on collective triumph. Every paddle stroke, every sail adjustment, propels us closer to that shared success, where the sum of our departmental efforts far exceeds the individual parts.

KPI vs OKR:

Having learnt the definitions of KPIs and OKR, how does this help discover a new perspective?

Maintaining yearly KPI goals for context, but measuring progress frequently, fosters an agile approach to improvement, allowing adjustments and optimizations throughout the year, not just in fixed review cycles.

Setting a context for the KPIs in an organisation is vital and while organisations look into this aspect, a timely pulse check will enable the org to stay relevant. Here is a guide to review the same:

- KPI cycle – Yearly.

- KPI definition – Half yearly.

- KPI review – Every Month/ Quarterly.

Below is comparison table of OKR and KPI

OKR	KPI
Goal achievement (qualitative assessment of progress)	Quantitative data (numbers, metrics)
Overall business outcomes	Department/team performance output
Set ambitious goals and drive strategic alignment	Track progress and identify areas for improvement

OKR	KPI
Goal achievement (qualitative assessment of progress)	Quantitative data (numbers, metrics)
Overall business outcomes	Department/team performance output
Typically shorter-term (quarterly or monthly)	Typically longer-term (annual or quarterly)
Destinations to strive for	Indicators of progress
Launch a new product, increase market share, improve employee engagement	Sales revenue, customer satisfaction rate, website traffic

KPI is an indicator OKR is destination

Here are the performance goals and measurements for each department, outlined as Objectives and Key Results (OKRs) with corresponding Key Performance Indicators (KPIs).:

Financial:

- I will increase revenue by X% as measured by:

  - Growing monthly recurring revenue (MRR) by X% each month.

  - Securing 5 new enterprise-level clients.

  - Upselling existing customers to higher-tier plans.

Customer:

- I will improve customer satisfaction by X% as measured by:

  - Increasing our Net Promoter Score (NPS) by 3 points.

- Reducing customer churn rate by X%.

- Increasing the average customer lifetime value (CLTV) by X%.

Product:

- I will launch 2 new products this year as measured by:

  - Releasing both products to market on time and within budget.

  - Achieving a X% adoption rate among target users within 3 months of launch.

  - Maintaining a product satisfaction rating of 4.5 out of 5 stars.

Marketing:

- I will increase website traffic by X% as measured by:

  - Generating 10,000 new organic visitors per month.

  - Growing social media followers by X% across all platforms.

  - Increasing brand awareness by X% as measured by online surveys.

Sales:

- I will close 100 deals this quarter as measured by:

  - Shortening the average sales cycle by 5 days.

- Increasing the win rate by X%.

- Expanding our customer base by X%.

Operations:

- I will reduce production costs by X% as measured by:

  - Negotiating better supplier contracts.

  - Optimizing production processes to reduce waste.

  - Improving inventory management to reduce carrying costs.

HR:

- I will increase employee engagement by X% as measured by:

  - Reducing employee turnover by X%.

  - Improving employee satisfaction scores by 2 points.

  - Increasing the number of employees participating in voluntary development programs

OKR and USER STORIES

One can easily infer that OKR cycle aligns with SCRUM framework's sprint cycle which is an explicit indicator of OKR and Agile partnership. One change Agile brings to OKR is Fixed goal chasing vs Iterative/ Dynamic Planning. A golden rule for business in the fast paced 21st century.

We cannot change customers but we have to change for customers.

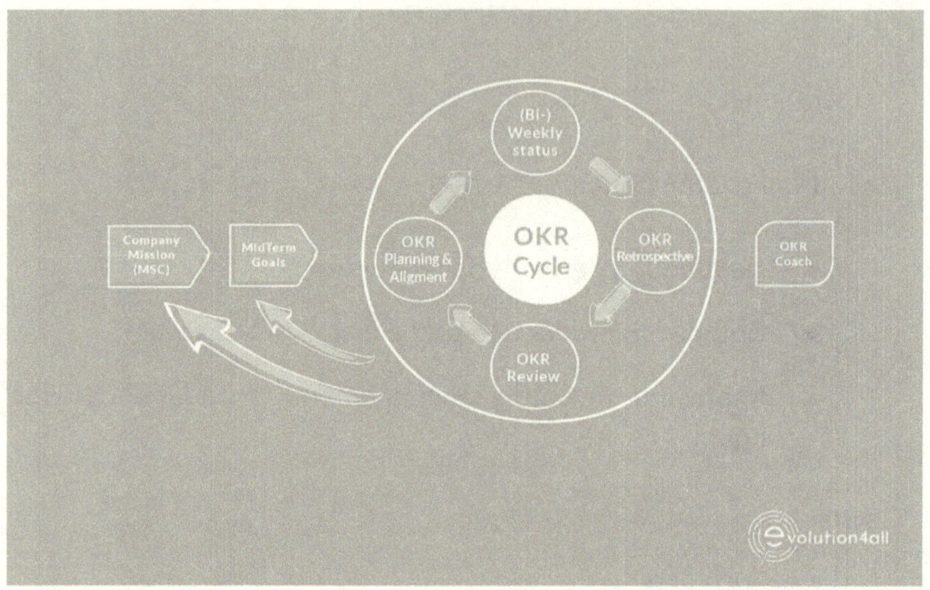

Measure What Matters: How Google, Bono, and the Gates Foundation Rock the World with OKRs by John E. Doerr teaches organizations and individuals how to implement a similar process by a different name. They call it objectives and key results, or OKRs for short. This powerful system is about to transform everything you know about productivity.

Best practice suggested:

Align your business OKR cycle with the team's Scrum cycle.

Also breakdown suitable OKR's Features EPICS—> user stories.

A dashboard can be created similar to Burn up chart to tract the user stories completed to achieve OKR.

It's interesting to infer the similarities of format used for OKR and user stories.

OKR format:

- I will (Objective) as measured by (this set of Key Results)

User story format:

- As a <User> I want <Need> so that <Result>

From organisationOKR's Each department could set their own KPI to create the Flow and also ensure that the

team metrics should be mapped with the KPI's eventually with organisationOKR's.

OKR—> KPI—>Agile Team metrics should be connected.

Well, it's a new message to connect OKR with agile team metrics, but is it possible? Yes because Agile and OKR share the same philosophy.

Lets see a quick analysis to understand the similarities between Agile and OKR

Layers	Culture	Strategy	Operations
Traditional	Top-down control	Annual planning	Water Fall
Agile Without OKR	Top down Control	Annual planning	Agile
Agile with OKR	Collective Leadership	Dynamic planning	Agile

Agile maturity assessment:

Agile maturity assessment is the measure Agile intrusion in various levels in organisation. An effective maturity assessment will help to enable the organisation's ability to adapt change in accordance with current market trends.

A survey on teams events, artefacts practice is the minimal assessment on agility but to highlight many agile coaches limit the agile maturity assessment by comparing the practices between teams, rather it should focus on agile mindset in all levels.

The Agile maturity assessment is not ready made, rather its bespoke approach. Based on overall organisational level agile maturity the assessment should be customised and rolled out to the teams.

Few things to remember on devising the assessment

- The assessment should not contain many Yes/No questions.

- Have a range of atleast 3-5 inputs from parties

- Ask the same question in two different formats to check the authenticity of answers which is usually followed in psychometric approach

A diverse set of business metrics are summarised below and plays a crucial role in assessing and optimising various functions. Here is a list of 16 metrics to help organisations track what matters:

- **Customer or User satisfaction gap** measures the difference between the customer's or user's desired experience and the actual experience they have with the product or service. This metric is important for understanding how well the business is meeting the needs of its customers.

- **Installed version index** measures the percentage of customers who are using the current version of the product. This metric is important for tracking the adoption of new features and for identifying any issues with older versions.

- **Release stabilisation period** measures the amount of time it takes for a new release of the product to become stable and reliable. This metric is important for ensuring that customers have a good experience with new features and for minimising the risk of disruptions.

- **On-product Index** measures the percentage of time that users spend using the product or service. This metric is important for understanding how engaged users are with the product and for identifying any areas of improvement.

- **Revenue per employee** measures the amount of revenue that each employee generates for the business. This metric is important for tracking the productivity of the workforce and identifying areas of further investment.

- **Revenue numbers** measure the total revenue that the business generates over a period of time. This metric is important for tracking the overall growth and profitability of the business.

- **Innovations vs innovators** measures the number of innovations that the business has produced compared to the number of employees who are considered innovators. This metric is important for assessing the organisation's culture of innovation and its ability to generate new ideas.

- **Customer satisfaction** measures how satisfied customers are with the company's products or services. This is a critical metric for any business, as it is directly correlated to customer loyalty and profitability.

- **Market share** is the percentage of the total market that a company controls. This metric is important for tracking the company's competitive position and identifying areas of

- **Revenue numbers** measure the total revenue that the company generates over a period of time. This metric is important for tracking the overall growth and profitability of the business.

- **Innovation rate** measures the number of new products or services that the company launches each year. This metric is important for assessing the company's ability to innovate and stay ahead of the competition.

- **Employee satisfaction** measures how satisfied employees are with their jobs and the company they work for. This is an important metric for any business, as employee satisfaction is directly correlated to employee productivity and retention.

- **Quality of life measures** the positive impact that the company has on the lives of its employees, customers, and the communities in which it operates. This can include factors such as job creation, charitable giving, and environmental protection.

- **Social impact measures** the company's positive impact on society. This can include factors such as diversity and inclusion, support for human rights, and ethical business practices.

- **Trust** measures how much customers and other stakeholders trust the company. This is an important asset for any business, as trust is essential for building long-term relationships with customers and partners.

- **Net impact on planet earth** measures the company's overall impact on the environment. This includes factors such as greenhouse gas emissions, water consumption, and waste production.

Metrics beyond numbers and generations:

Forget the cold grip of spreadsheets and the sterile hum of algorithms. Let's dive into the future of measurement, where numbers become windows into hearts and minds, where generations converse through shared understanding, and where success is painted not on a sterile canvas, but on the vibrant mural of human connection.

Social impact and net impact on planet Earth are increasingly important to businesses and consumers alike. Businesses are realising that they need to take responsibility for their social and environmental impact in order to be successful in the long term. Consumers are also more aware of the impact of their purchases and are choosing to support businesses that have a positive social and environmental impact.

There are a number of ways that businesses can improve their social and net impact on planet Earth. Some examples include:

- Hiring from disadvantaged groups

- Investing in employee training and development

- Sourcing materials from sustainable suppliers

- Reducing waste and pollution

- Using renewable energy

- Donating to charities and social causes

By taking these steps and more, businesses can make a positive impact in the world and create a more sustainable future for all.

Here are some specific examples of businesses that are making a positive social and net impact on planet Earth:

- Patagonia is a clothing company that is committed to environmental sustainability. They use recycled materials in their products and donate 1% of their sales to environmental causes.

- TOMS is a shoe company that gives away a pair of shoes to a child in need for every pair of shoes they sell.

- Method is a cleaning products company that uses non-toxic ingredients and donates to environmental charities.

- B Lab is a non-profit organisation that certifies businesses that meet high standards of social and environmental performance, accountability, and transparency.

Oil & Natural Gas Corporation (ONGC) signed a memorandum with M/s Greenko ZeroC Private Limited (Greenko), in July of 2022, to work together and explore environmentally friendly opportunities for producing green ammonia and other derivatives of green hydrogen. The National Hydrogen Mission seeks to establish India as a global hub for green hydrogen.

Tamil Nadu Newsprints and Papers Limited (TNPL): In the pulp and paper sector, Tamil Nadu Newsprints and Papers Limited, was ahead of its time, earning the Green Business Leadership Award in the year 2009-2010 - which included a wind farm project and two clean development mechanism projects that has shown good results of saving the environment.

These are just a few examples of the many businesses that are making a positive difference in the world. By partnering with these businesses, consumers contribute to creating a sustainable future for all.

"A program's business metrics should be rooted in its roadmap."

- Anonymous.

Overall, business agility metrics are an important tool for any business that wants to sustain agility and success. By tracking the right metrics over time and using the data to drive improvement, businesses can achieve their goals and objectives more effectively.

To download a sample Agile maturity assessment, please visit www.agilebodhi.com.

Beyond the sprint: Agile program management:

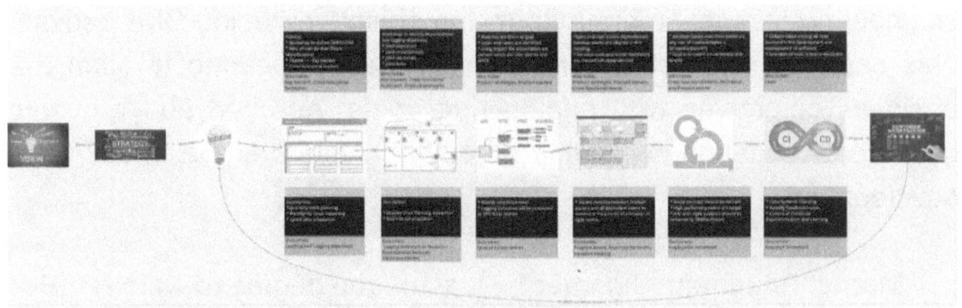

Agile program management practices vary widely across organizations. To address this, this book proposes the below framework that business metrics can guide Agile execution and scaling at the program level. By providing a structured methodology, organizations can effectively adopt Agile practices to enhance program delivery. Program managers are key facilitators, advised to be involved right from the start of this framework, till receiving the feedback from customers of Initiatives execution.

Break the Org Vision into Initiatives:

The foundation of a successful program begins with a clear understanding of its purpose and alignment with organizational goals. It is crucial to ensure the program is strategically aligned with the organization's overall direction. Initiatives are born by slicing the Org vision into implementable initiatives. Closed feedback loop approach in frequent rhythms through Market research, competitor analysis, Customer feedback and innovation can also lead to create initiatives apart from Org initiatives.

Metric: Vision Clarity Index: Measure the extent to which initiatives directly contribute to achieving the organizational vision.

Initiatives goes for OKR/OGSM planning workshop

OKR workshop is for Key business owners from Product and engineering leaders to brainstorm the objectives using OKR canvas. This could be a quarterly or lesser frequency meeting to align the business objectives with engineering goals. As cited above in this chapter, OKR definition should align with Agile method of software development

Metric: Roadmap Alignment: Measure the degree to which OKRs/ OGSMs are aligned with the overall program roadmap and strategic objectives.

Leadership alignment mapping

Leadership alignment meetings are essential to identify the Joint objectives, commitment, resources and risk with the respective teams with leaders which makes the teams understand the goal and leaders to provide necessary support for the teams.

Metric: Executive Sponsorship: Measure the level of active support and involvement from executive leadership in the program.

Impact mapping/ Story slicing workshops

The struggle of breaking the business needs to smaller user stories are still a potential challenge in the industry. This book recommends the tool Impact Mapping. It was introduced to the world by Gojko Adzic in 2012 in his book Impact Mapping. This is very useful to bring vertical sliced user stories to the team with clear acceptance criteria which solves Major problems in Agile delivery. Metric: Story Slicing Accuracy: Evaluate the effectiveness of story slicing in breaking down features into smaller User stories.

Team alignment mapping

Dependencies are often a major bottleneck for Agile teams. Program managers should have a closer look towards dependencies using rhythmic Team alignment mapping. Identifying and addressing the dependencies of initiatives are a paramount exercise which should be done by Product and engineering counterparts.

Metric: Dependency Matrix: Create a visual representation of dependencies between teams and measure the average time it takes to resolve a dependency.

Apart from Agile execution on the team level the above practices could be helpful for scaling agile in the program layer. To ensure Agile program success, each practice should be supported by defined metrics. These metrics, aligned with the program's roadmap, will provide valuable insights into progress, identify areas for improvement, and ultimately drive business outcomes.

Chapter 5

Conclusion

Are metrics agile or anti-agile?

The essential inquiry is whether metrics are aligned with or contrary to Agile principles. Metrics, in and of themselves, do not possess an inherent agility or anti-agility. Metrics is a double sided sword. It is the manner in which metrics are employed and the context in which they are utilised that defines their compatibility or misalignment with Agile principles.

Metrics in agile way:

Context is king: Agile values adaptability and continuous improvement. Metrics should reflect focus ont:

Progress *over* perfection

Learning *over* blame.

Flow *over* output

Transparency fosters accountability: Agile thrives on open communication and shared responsibility. Metrics should be transparently displayed and discussed, empowering teams to own their improvement.

Small batches, big insights: Agile embraces frequent feedback loops and short iterations. Metrics should be readily available and actionable, providing insights within the same iteration they're collected.

People over processes: Agile prioritises the well-being and motivation of individuals. Metrics should never become a burden or create undue pressure, hindering team morale and creativity.

Quality at every step: While Agile emphasises speed, it doesn't compromise on quality. Metrics should track defect rates, code coverage, and user satisfaction alongside delivery speed.

Embrace retrospectives: Agile uses retrospectives to learn from successes and failures. Metrics should inform these discussions, helping teams identify areas for improvement.

Metrics for improvement, not punishment: Agile promotes a culture of continuous learning. Metrics should serve as tools for identifying opportunities of growth, not instruments for finger-pointing or punitive actions.

Celebrate progress, not just goals: Agile emphasises the journey over the destination. Metrics should acknowledge and celebrate incremental progress, boosting team morale and motivation.

Adapt and evolve: Agile thrives on dynamic environments. Metrics should be flexible and adaptable, evolving alongside the team's needs and priorities.

Apply Metrics in Anti-Agile pattern:

"Metrics Misapplication" versus "Agile" isn't exactly a battle between two opposing forces, but rather a mismatch between intentions and outcomes. While metrics themselves are neutral tools, their misapplication can seriously clash with the core principles of Agile.

Here's how:

Micromanagement through Metrics: Bombarding teams with excessive, granular metrics can breed a culture of anxiety, stifle creativity, and hinder intrinsic motivation. Agile needs self-organising teams, not metric-driven robots.

Punitive Use of Metrics: Turning metrics into instruments for blame or pressure can damage team morale and trust, fostering a fear-based environment that cripples collaboration and adaptability.

Metrics Blindness to Context: Applying generic metrics across different contexts and situations ignores the unique nature of each project and team. Agile demands flexibility and tailoring approaches to specific circumstances.

Overemphasis on Productivity Metrics: Placing exclusive focus on output metrics, such as lines of code or completed tasks, rather than prioritising outcomes and delivered value, goes against Agile principles.

Excessive Emphasis on Reporting: An overly heightened focus on collecting and reporting metrics can be counter to agile practices, introducing unnecessary overhead and diminishing the time available for value delivery.

The key is to use metrics wisely, making sure they match Agile values. Metrics should serve the goal of delivering value and improving the process, not becoming an end in themselves.

Measure and improve are very much cited in the below Agile principles:

- **7th Principle:** Working software is the primary measure of progress.

- **9th Principle:** Continuous attention to technical excellence and good design enhances agility.

- **12th Principle:** At regular intervals, the team reflects on how to become more effective, then tunes and adjusts its behaviour accordingly we can summarise the message from Agile principle for metrics in simple words; Using Agile Value which states: "Working software over comprehensive documentation'

In the IT industry, directly quantifying individual productivity can be challenging. However, a more effective approach involves assessing productivity based on the value generated over time.

Implementing metrics is vital for any system, however understanding the pain areas of that very system enables the implementation.

Below we discuss the Pain areas of Metrics and potential solutions:

1. Unavailability of Updated Data in the Tool:

- Streamline Data Entry: Integrate data collection into daily workflows using automated processes or user-friendly interfaces.

- Review Data Quality: Regularly assess data accuracy and completeness, addressing any inconsistencies or gaps.

- Centralize Data Storage: Ensure a single, accessible source for all metrics data, promoting visibility and consistency.

- Perceived Lack of Usefulness:

- Align Metrics with Objectives: Ensure metrics directly support business goals (OKR) and team priorities, fostering relevance and buy-in.

- Involve Teams in Selection: Engage teams in choosing metrics they find meaningful and actionable, increasing ownership and engagement.

- Provide Context and Interpretation: Explain the purpose of metrics and how they inform decision-making, fostering understanding and buy-in.

- Variance in Agile Understanding and Compliance:

- Conduct Agile Training: Provide comprehensive training on Agile principles and practices, including metrics usage and information radiators.

- Facilitate Cross-Team Collaboration: Encourage knowledge sharing and consistency through regular meetings and communities of practice.

- Enforce Data Maintenance: Establish clear guidelines and expectations for keeping information radiators and dashboards updated.

- Progress Reporting to Top Management:

- Tailor Reports to Audience: Present metrics in a way that resonates with top management, focusing on key outcomes and business impact.

- Contextualize Data: Explain trends and patterns, offering insights and potential actions rather than just numbers.

- Visualize Progress: Use compelling charts and dashboards to highlight key metrics and communicate progress effectively.

- Tool Usability Challenges:

- Evaluate Tool Fit: Assess if the current tool aligns with team needs and workflows, exploring alternatives if necessary.

- Provide Training and Support: Offer ongoing training and support to ensure team members are comfortable using the tool effectively.

- Seek User Feedback: Regularly collect feedback on tool usability and functionality, identifying areas for improvement.

- Promote a Culture of Data-Driven Decision-Making: Foster a mindset that values metrics as tools for continuous improvement, not just reporting.

- Emphasize Transparency and Open Communication: Share metrics openly and discuss them regularly, encouraging collaboration and learning.

- Regularly Review and Adapt: Periodically assess the effectiveness of metrics and tools, making adjustments as needed to ensure they remain relevant and valuable.

- By addressing these challenge points and fostering a culture of effective metrics usage, you can unlock the potential of data to drive continuous improvement, alignment, and success within your Agile teams.

Considering a baseline for metrics enables effectiveness of its usage. Here's a guide on how to baseline a metric:

1. **Define the Metric:**

   - Clearly articulate what you want to measure based on FOCUS criteria, introduced in chapter 1. Ensure it aligns with your overall goals and objectives.

2. **Gather Historical Data:**

   - Collect relevant data for a sufficient period. The duration depends on the metric's nature and expected variability (e.g., weeks for website traffic, months for sales figures).

3. **Calculate the Baseline:**

   - Choose an appropriate statistical measure:

     - *Mean:* Average value over the period.

- ◎ *Median:* Middle value when data is ordered.

- ◎ *Mode:* Most frequent value.

- Consider seasonality or trends when calculating (e.g., use a baseline for the same quarter last year).

4. **Establish Target Values:**

   - Set realistic yet ambitious targets for improvement based on the baseline.

   - Consider industry benchmarks or historical performance.

   - Ensure targets are aligned with the overall business strategy.

5. **Monitor and Review:**

   - Analyze trends and patterns to identify areas for improvement and regularly review and adjust the baseline as needed due to changes in business processes or goals.

Baselines are not static—they should evolve as your business and goals change. Regular review and adaptation are crucial for ensuring metrics remain relevant and actionable.

Based on the "Agile: Measure what Matters" survey, a concise summary of the widely applied top 10 Key Metrics:

1. **Velocity:** Measures the amount of work a team can complete within a set time period.

2. **Say-Do Ratio:** Tracks the percentage of commitments that are actually delivered.

3. **#Defects:** Counts the number of errors or bugs found in a product or service.

4. **Release Efficiency:** Assesses the overall effectiveness of releases, considering factors like timeliness, quality, and impact.

5. **Cycle Time:** Measures how long it takes to complete a task, from start to finish.

6. **Effort:** Measures the amount of work required to complete tasks, often expressed in hours or person-days.

7. **Volume of Outputs:** Quantifies the total amount of work produced, such as the number of features or products delivered.

8. **Story Points:** Estimates the relative complexity of work items, used for planning and tracking progress.

9. **Code Coverage:** Measures the percentage of code that is tested by automated tests.

10. **NPS (Net Promoter Score):** Gauges customer satisfaction and loyalty.

While the above lists look impressive, focusing solely on team metrics provides a limited view of performance. In the above list except NPS, the other metrics revolve in team level only. While team-level metrics are valuable for understanding individual team dynamics and efficiency, they often lack context in terms of the bigger picture. To gain a comprehensive understanding of success, it's crucial to incorporate org-wide and business-level metrics alongside team metrics.

Common mistakes in metrics is summarised in tabular column format with alternatives suggested:

Dysfunctions in metrics	Alternatives for the same
Measuring only team metrics, neglecting org and business levels.	Utilize org-wide metrics for overall growth.

Focusing solely on lagging indicators, ignoring leading indicators.	Include leading indicators like cycle time, velocity, and say-do ratio.
Data collected but not acted upon.	IEstablish a rhythmic tracking system with regular reviews and adjustments.
Metrics measured by someone else, not the team itself.	Foster ownership and accountability by allowing teams to record, compare, and ideate on their own metrics.
Overwhelmed by too many metrics.	Prioritize and focus on a few key metrics that align with goals.
Metrics treated as absolutes, not contextually.	Consider external factors and historical trends when interpreting data.
Team metrics used for individual performance reviews.	Use team-level metrics for team improvement, individual metrics for IndividualIndividual growth.
Ridgid tools hampering agility.	Employ agile tools that adapt to changing needs and priorities.

Sean Ellis coined the term "North Star metric" and it's a great idea. Having too many metrics vs one important metric called north star metric is very useful for the growth of org, teams and business.

The key lies in striking a balance between having sufficient metrics to monitor progress and avoiding excessive data collection that can hinder productivity. Instead of prescribing a specific number of metrics, it's crucial to focus on selecting metrics that are relevant to the project's objectives and provide actionable insights. By carefully evaluating the relevance of metrics regularly and communicating findings effectively, teams can optimise their metric tracking approach to enhance project success.

Define your North star metrics for team, organisation and business based on FOCUS.

We've explored the dynamic interplay between metrics and Agile practices. We've discovered that, when used thoughtfully and in alignment with Agile values, metrics become powerful allies in the pursuit of excellence. They are not adversaries but rather essential tools that guide, inform, and support Agile teams on their journey toward continuous improvement.

As we conclude this journey through the world of software Agile metrics, it is evident that they can be a force for good in the software industry. By understanding the nuanced relationship between metrics and Agile, you're better equipped to navigate the complexities of modern software development, ensuring that your teams not only embrace Agile practices but also leverage metrics as a compass, guiding them toward successful, customer-focused outcomes.

While data-driven decision making is undeniably logical and efficient, combining data with intuition (data-informed decisions) can be a powerful and successful approach. Many successful ventures have thrived on this potent combination, as it fosters growth by leveraging both objective analysis and valuable human experience. May your journey through the world of software Agile metrics be enlightening, empowering, and, above all, a catalyst for your organisation's continued success in this ever-evolving field.

www.ingramcontent.com/pod-product-compliance
Lightning Source LLC
Chambersburg PA
CBHW031743150726
47989CB00006B/2576